ONE-MINUTE

Bible Inspirations

for WOMEN

ELIZABETH GEORGE

HARVEST HOUSE PUBLISHERS
EUGENE, OREGON

Cover design by Studio Gearbox, Chris Gilbert

Cover Photo © OKing / Shutterstock

Interior design by Rockwell Davis

Italics in Scripture quotations indicate author emphasis.

Harvest House Publishers has made every effort to trace the ownership of all poems and quotes. In the event of a question arising from the use of a poem or quote, we regret any error made and will be pleased to make the necessary correction in future editions of this book.

For bulk, special sales, or ministry purchases, please call 1-800-547-8979. Email: Customerservice@hhpbooks.com

M This logo is a federally registered trademark of the Hawkins Children's LLC. Harvest House Publishers, Inc., is the exclusive licensee of this trademark.

Material includes content adapted from *Moments of Grace for a Woman's Heart, One-Minute Inspirations for Women*, and *A Woman Who Reflects the Heart of Jesus* by Elizabeth George.

One-Minute Bible Inspirations for Women

Copyright © 2009, 2010, 2013 by Elizabeth George
Published by Harvest House Publishers
Eugene, Oregon 97408
www.harvesthousepublishers.com

ISBN 978-0-73-69-8283-2 (pbk)
ISBN 978-0-73-69-8284-9 (eBook)

Library of Congress Control Number: 2021949968

Printed in China

22 23 24 25 26 27 28 29 30 / RDS / 10 9 8 7 6 5 4 3 2 1

A Note from Elizabeth

You and I have so much to be thankful for because we have the Bible. In it Jesus teaches us what perfect humanity is, and then He lives it for us. He isn't an untouchable superstar. Our Lord is our companion and our model as we make a prayerful, faithful effort to live God's way. Biblical standards that seem so hard for us are clearly seen in Him. Because He shows us the way as a fellow human, we can follow Him with confidence and conviction and live out the qualities He possessed.

Isn't it incredible that our Savior experienced all that we experience as humans, including hunger, thirst, weariness, love, sadness, and even anger, yet without sin? My prayer is that as you read these devotions inspired by God's Word and the life of Jesus, they'll encourage you as a woman who seeks to demonstrate His grace, love, and obedience in every circumstance.

Let's begin this great journey to renew your heart and mind so you can know the perfect will of God and live it with great joy and gratitude. Praise Him!

Elizabeth George

Simple Success

Where does God have you today? What roles and responsibilities has the Lord given you? And how about your dreams and your heart's desires? Many of these questions and their answers indicate God's directions for your life. That's why I am encouraging you to take time to discover what the Bible says about your roles…and then pray about them.

God's road to success is quite simple: As you faithfully follow Him with all your heart and are obedient to fulfill His will for you, you will be blessed. You will enjoy success. Yes, you're human and will have moments when you fail, fall down, or stay in one place for a while. But as you rely on God and do what He asks of you through His Word and prayer, He will give you the desire and confidence—and power—to move on and enjoy life in Him.

> *Lord, as I look into Your Word, my heart is*
> *moved. Open my eyes to Your will. Strengthen*
> *me to step out on the path to greater faithfulness*
> *so I can better carry out Your will. Bless*
> *me in the ways You choose. Amen.*

Reflecting God's Light

Your desires and choices as one who walks in the light are governed by your prior determination to please God and not yourself. When you do this and bear the fruit of goodness, righteousness, and truthfulness, you reflect His light to those in darkness. God says,

> You are the light of the world. A city that is set on a hill cannot be hidden. Nor do they light a lamp and put it under a basket, but on a lampstand, and it gives light to all who are in the house. Let your light so shine before men, that they may see your good works and glorify your Father in heaven (Matthew 5:14-16).

Imagine! Just as you are able to physically assist someone in the dark by giving them a flashlight, you are able to help others as you reflect the light that is yours as a child of the Supreme Light.

Lord, I walk in Your light with gratitude and
awe. I desire to share Your light with the world
by making righteous and holy decisions. Use
me, Lord, so that I can glorify You. Amen.

Looking Up for Hope

The hope we derive from the promise of Jesus' coming helps us to wait patiently. When He arrives, He will set everything in order. He will make things right. He will correct all abuses. He will bring deliverance from our suffering. Let the certainty of the Lord's return encourage your heart as you endure hard times, moments that seem endless, and the unknowns of tomorrow.

Where is your gaze fixed? Downward…on the suffering you must endure? Or upward…in the direction from which Jesus will come? Your patience will be helped when you trust the promise of His return. You and I live with "what is," but we have the promise of "what is to be." And in-between is the waiting. You can fret, worry, and pace…or you can put on a heart of patience (Colossians 3:12 NASB). Which will it be?

> Lord, I'm making the decision to be still and
> to trust in Your promises. Today is hard, but I
> will wait for the rain of Your love to fall upon
> me. I will wait with hope for Your grace to
> show me the way You want me to go. Amen.

Trust God for All of Life

Whenever your life seems to be out of control or you feel like the world and its pressures are crashing in on you, realize and remember God is sovereign. He is in charge, and He is a faithful, flawless administrator. He is working out His good and acceptable and perfect will. His purpose in saving you and showering a continuing multitude of blessings upon you has been established.

As God's own dear child, your day and your future are secure in Him due to His kindness and mercy. God's blessings are yours! Your heart's response to God's plan of redemption for you will always be one of reveling in the truth and giving unending praise and thanksgiving to Him for all He has and will give you "according to the riches of His grace" (Ephesians 1:7).

> *Lord, as I look into Your Word, I want to thank You*
> *for Your concern and care for the details of my life.*
> *Today has its difficulties and stress. May I be faithful*
> *to trust in Your perfect and personal management*
> *of the world around me…and me! Amen.*

Your Precious Privilege

Pursuing godliness is all about Jesus Christ. He is the mystery of godliness, the mystery once hidden but *is* now revealed. As a believer in Christ and as a woman after God's own heart, you have the ability—and the precious privilege—to live for Him and strive to be like Him.

Yes, you *can* live a godly life in and through Jesus Christ. Put plainly and simply, this is *piety*, a deep-seated loyalty and devotion to Christ that affects your conduct and commitment to spiritual duties and practices. What a wonderful reality, and what a wonderful possession to share with others! May you and I never let the passing of time crowd out this amazing message of the awesome mystery of Christ—the hope of glory—in us. As a woman pursuing godliness, please don't lose sight of the truth and power of the gospel of Jesus Christ.

> *Lord, I'm so thankful to grow in faith as the mystery of godliness is revealed in Jesus Christ. What a tremendous gift to be part of the living, growing, believing church that serves You. Thank You. Amen.*

Blessing and a Cure

Consider the many riches God has lavished upon you. You were lost and without hope, but God in His great mercy forgave your sins through His Son's death on your behalf. Then, wonder of wonders, you were taken into God's own family and given the status of a daughter!

Why not pause and reflect on why God's blessings are a cure for any Christian (including you) who entertains a low self-image or "poor me" attitude? Praise God for His plan for you. Devote yourself to fulfilling His purposes. Show the world your true worth and identity as His child "to the praise of the glory of His grace" (Ephesians 1:6).

Lord, as I look into Your Word, I thank You from the depths of my heart for the many spiritual blessings You've given me through Your Son Jesus. Help me recall them when I put myself down, when I think I'm inferior, and when I feel sorry for myself. Amen.

Your Conduct Is Your Witness

God calls us to a life of honorable conduct. The Greek word for *honorable* is rich in meaning and implies the purest, highest, and noblest kind of goodness. To live honorably means to live in a way that is so clean that no charges against us can stand up. Gracious, upright behavior will always be our greatest defense…and our greatest witness.

> Beloved, I beg you as sojourners and pilgrims, abstain from fleshly lusts which war against the soul, having your conduct honorable among the Gentiles, that when they speak against you as evildoers, they may, by your good works which they observe, glorify God in the day of visitation (1 Peter 2:11-12).

Mistreatment and misunderstandings *will* come, but how you handle them speaks of your faith. Your conduct, lived out in a holy lifestyle, commends Christ to others around you.

God, I've always viewed the world's opposition to my beliefs as an obstacle instead of an opportunity. Please give me patience and a spirit of perseverance so I can overcome mistreatments and misunderstandings in ways that lead others to a desire to know, understand, and glorify You. Amen.

God Provides Every Time

What situation do you face today? Has someone you love fallen sick? Are you concerned about your child's behavior? Do you hold on to a hurt from the past? Just as Christ's strength is sufficient for all you endure, it is sufficient to get you through each day.

As His child you can look to Jesus, His Word, His promises, and His strength, and He will graciously—every time and without fail!—provide what you need for taking one more step along your God-ordained path. In fact, tell yourself, "I can do *all* things [including this] through Christ who strengthens me" (Philippians 4:13). How blessed you are to be able to turn to and trust God in every circumstance for every need.

Lift up these words as your personal promise. There is no need to merely cope when you have the Lord!

> *God, I give today's trouble to You. With renewed hope I want to exchange my independence for God-dependence. I want to stop striving to be self-sufficient so I can embrace the hope and peace of being God-sufficient. Amen.*

Seek a Spiritual Savior

In the dramatic ending of the Gospel of Luke, we can read about the final week of Jesus' life on earth. In fact, our Lord had prepared for this specific time. Even at age 12 Jesus knew His purpose: "Did you not know that I must be about My Father's business?" (Luke 2:49). Three years after Jesus began His ministry at the age of 30, Jesus had inflamed a nation with His passion, His teachings, and His miraculous healing of others. And He also consistently angered the Jewish religious leaders.

Yet as Jesus entered Jerusalem, He wept because He knew the Jewish people were not looking for a spiritual Savior. They were looking for a conquering hero who would return their nation to glory. Are you searching for meaning in the right places? Are you looking for Someone to make your life meaningful today and for eternity? Recognize and embrace Christ as your Messiah!

Lord, I want to serve and honor You in everything I do. Help me love those who don't know You. Give me the wisdom to share with them what will give them peace now and forever—give them You! Amen.

Meditate on These Things

Aren't we blessed? The Bible provides the clear-cut instruction our hearts yearn for. It also reveals how we should live and what to pay attention to in our lives.

> Whatever things are true, whatever things are noble, whatever things are just, whatever things are pure, whatever things are lovely, whatever things are of good report, if there is any virtue and if there is anything praiseworthy—meditate on these things (Philippians 4:8).

I know you want your life that is spent here on earth to mean something and to bring glory to God. Thank the Lord for showing you *how* in His Word!

> *Father, I look to You for Your grace and Your strength. As I live in the shadow of eternity, please help me embrace all that today offers that has its roots in You. I want to learn more about You, to serve and love others more, and to offer my praise to You every day. Amen.*

Think on These

Our perspectives and attitudes and hearts change when we meditate on what is important to our faith, growth, and intimacy with God. When you are out and about, here are three ways to focus your thoughts.

Meditate on God. When we contemplate the person of God and His attributes, we're pondering the riches of His wisdom, knowledge, goodness, and grace to us.

Think about Jesus Christ. Reflect on the Gospel accounts of the life of Christ: His nativity, His death, His resurrection, His ascension.

Think about the Word of God. As the psalmist declared, the law of the Lord is perfect, sure, right, pure, clean, true, righteous…and sweeter than honey and the honeycomb (Psalm 19:7-10).

When we spend our time thinking on these three lofty "things"—God, His Son, and His Word—why would we want to think on anything else?

> *Lord, I worship You today. As I seek a*
> *peace-filled life, I will meditate on those*
> *things that are Your truth, that are good*
> *and holy. May the fruit of my thoughts and*
> *life be praiseworthy in Your eyes. Amen.*

Where Does Your Treasure Go?

Do you want to learn about how you relate to money? It's going to one specific source—your checking account. Your attitude and priorities are right there in black and white. Ask yourself: Am I a spender? A giver? A hoarder? A saver?

Did your "treasure" go to some online shops...or to help people? Was your treasure spent for curtains...or for the church? You may be surprised to find that your spending doesn't always reflect the heart of love and sharing you want to have.

God may not be asking you to sell or give away all of your possessions and wealth. But He is definitely asking you to prayerfully consider how you handle the riches He has given you. You are *so* blessed because now you can bless others.

God, help me be a cheerful giver. I want to honor
You with my attitudes and actions regarding how
I spend and share the financial and material
blessings You have given me. Please remind
me and help me release my hold on earthly
treasures. I know my heart will reap the rewards
of joyously giving in Your name. Amen.

Peace Will Prevail

Joy and peace rank high when we list what we want. And in God's inspired Word we have the source of both joy and peace! To embrace these desired qualities, we are to do two things.

Rejoice. This is not optional, my friend. This is a command: "Rejoice in the Lord always. Again I will say, rejoice!" (Philippians 4:4). We are to rejoice *in the Lord*, no matter what is happening to us.

Pray. This, too, is a command. Rather than suffering from anxiety, we are to present our needs to the Lord and trust Him to provide for us. When we do this we will experience "the peace of God"—the peace that is characteristic of God Himself. Even when difficult circumstances don't change, God's peace will prevail. It will protect us against the anxieties and worries that attack our hearts and minds.

Lord, I'm ready to create a "to-do list" of joy and peace. I lift up my needs to You and trust in You. You calm my fears, guide my steps, and lead me to Your presence. I am rejoicing in You right now! Amen.

Giving Thanks

When Paul was a prisoner, he wrote a letter to his friends in Ephesus saying, "I also, after I heard of your faith in the Lord Jesus and your love for all the saints, do not cease to give thanks for you, making mention of you in my prayers" (Ephesians 1:15-16). You would expect an innocent prisoner to rant, rave, blame others, question God, and sink into deep depression. But not Paul. Paul praised God!

Pray as Paul did! No matter what your circumstances or your troubles are, give thanks and express gratitude for the people in your life and for the body of Christ.

Why not write a few words of hope and comfort to a loved one who needs encouragement? Or call someone and pray with them about their needs for God's peace. Share spiritual insights from God's Word.

Lord, thank You for hearing my prayers for my friends, for me, and for those who don't know You. Help me be an example of Your love and grace. And for those friends who know You, I pray they will see Your hand in their lives. Amen.

No Playing Favorites

We might think we are fair to everyone, but partiality can easily sneak into our attitudes and behaviors. When it does, it can prevent us from living our faith.

> If there should come into your assembly a man with gold rings, in fine apparel, and there should also come in a poor man in filthy clothes, and you pay attention to the one wearing the fine clothes and say to him, "You sit here in a good place," and say to the poor man, "You stand there," or, "Sit here at my footstool," have you not shown partiality among yourselves, and become judges with evil thoughts? (James 2:2-4).

Favoritism is incompatible with our salvation, which was accomplished by an impartial God who extended His love toward all of us by sending His Son to die for our sins and redeem us. Let His pure love guide your actions, thoughts, and relationships every day.

Father, I don't want to show favoritism because
of perceived wealth, success, or influence.
Keep me from becoming jaded by the world's
standards. Give me a heart for all people
so I can tell them about You. Amen.

Gathering Eternal Treasures

Everyone wonders about life after death. In the Gospel of Luke, we have a parable Jesus told that gives us a glimpse of life beyond this earth. In that parable a beggar died and entered a life of comfort after an earthly existence of torment. We also read about the death of a rich man who lived his days on earth in splendor…and woke up to eternal torment in Hades. What made the difference? We can infer that the rich man did not seek or heed the instruction of God. He didn't reach out to help the poor and downtrodden. Instead, he concentrated on gathering worldly wealth. The beggar, Lazarus, was humble and content to eat what fell from the rich man's table. When Lazarus died, he was rewarded by being brought into heaven.

My friend, clearly the ultimate stewardship you are given is your life on earth. How can you use it to be a better servant of God and to glorify Him? Here is a prayer that can help you.

God, I want to be rich in good works for You.
Replace my longing for earthly treasures with hope
and peace and a desire for heavenly blessings. Amen.

Chosen by God

Doesn't it stand to reason that what's on the inside should and must come out? When God comes to live in us, shouldn't our lives change? And when we contemplate the price Jesus Christ paid for our redemption, shouldn't this result in faithful obedience to Him? Scripture reveals all that is given to us and all that happens to us on the inside when we are born again—the new birth, the inheritance, and the fact that we are kept for heaven and heaven is kept for us. Such wonders should make a radical difference in us.

As a Christian you have been granted a position in Christ. You are called to God, chosen by God, saved by God, and declared holy as belonging to God. As a woman after God's own heart, set your mind to work on incorporating His divine likeness in your life today.

Lord, I want to make Your characteristics my own. I want to make my actions and words honor Your love and sacrifice. Your presence and grace have transformed me. Out of gratitude, I pray to be faithful and obedient to Your calling. Amen.

Wisdom for Life

The Bible gives you and me straightforward direction about our conduct. Here are a few dos and don'ts to take to heart:

- *Do* examine your own life.
- *Do* pursue godliness.
- *Do* pray for purity in your leadership.
- *Do* trust God with the lives and actions of others.
- *Don't* be a part of causing trouble in the church.
- *Don't* be a part of gossiping and tearing down the hard-won reputations of others.

Make sure you put your time and commitments toward actions and words that are good. May those be revealed in time as the fruits of a faithful life.

> *God, there are people in my life who are*
> *watching my behavior. I am responsible for*
> *the example of Christ they are witnessing.*
> *Help me practice godly, principled behavior*
> *so I can serve You with integrity. Amen.*

Living in Unity

Euodia and Syntyche, two of Paul's friends and coworkers for the cause of Christ, were having differences, and the rift between them was affecting those around them. So how did Paul handle the problem?

Paul spoke directly to the two women and implored them to settle their dispute and live in harmony. He asked that they "be of the same mind in the Lord" (Philippians 4:2), that they keep the peace, and that they live in love. They were to put aside their differences for the grander cause of the common good of the church at Philippi and the body of Christ. My friend, pray that you won't be the cause of any disruptions in your church and that you *will not* hinder the work of the church for the cause of Christ. Ask God to help you live in unity.

> *God, please keep me from causing division in Your body of believers. Help me follow Paul's words and actions that bring unity and harmony to those around me. I want to be a peacekeeper. Amen.*

Ready for Your Makeover?

Your Master is calling you to action. He wants you to stop living a purposeless life. You have been miraculously raised from the dead! There is no need or reason to live as those who are unsaved. You are to live as the daughter of the King of kings! And you don't have to do this in your own strength. Jesus will help you…if you only ask! So start each morning by talking to Him and asking Him to guide you and give you strength to live for Him. Leave the old life behind. Study God's Word and incorporate His wisdom and principles into your daily life. And don't be surprised when you might not recognize yourself after this makeover!

Lord, I am a new creation in You. But I have held on to some sins, failures, and worldly attitudes. Wrap me in the wonderful fabric of Your nature and Your love. Help me become a new woman in You. Thank You. Amen.

Tell Others What God Has Done

In Luke 8, there is an account of a man who was kept shackled and under guard. Finally, he broke loose and was living in the wilderness and running around naked. He was in a hopeless condition. Then he met Jesus, and Jesus commanded the unclean spirits to leave the man's body. As a result, he was healed!

The changed man wanted to stay with Jesus, but he submitted to the Lord's authority when Jesus said, "Return to your own house, and tell what great things God has done for you." Full of new passion and appreciation, "he went his way and proclaimed throughout the whole city what great things Jesus had done for him" (verse 39).

Are you faithfully submitting to authority and following through on one of your purposes—that of telling others about Christ? Ask Jesus to revitalize your passion for sharing what He has done in your life.

> *Lord, I will tell of the great things You*
> *have done for me. Please reveal the areas*
> *in my life that need to change. Amen.*

Gratitude for Teachers

Every now and then it's good to pause and remember those who have faithfully and accurately taught you. You can also thank God for teachers who take great risks to instruct others. As James 3:1 says, "My brethren, let not many of you become teachers, knowing that we shall receive a stricter judgment."

Take time to bless…

- *Your pastor.* Thank God for your pastor's diligent study as he seeks to clearly teach God's truths.
- *Your parents.* What skills, values, and instructions for life did they impart?
- *Schoolteachers and professors.* God uses these dedicated souls to enlighten our lives.
- *Older women.* Mentors take time to encourage, instruct, and train you in the godly way to go.

When it's your turn to encourage someone, ask God to give you "the tongue of the learned" so you can freely give a word of support and instruction to those who are weary (Isaiah 50:4).

Lord, thank You for those who modeled faith and godly wisdom to me during my life. If, with Your leading, I have an opportunity to shepherd another person, I will take that calling seriously. Please grant me Your wisdom. Amen.

Faithful in All Things

Is faithfully serving God one of the deep-seated desires of your heart? Faithfulness is a beautiful quality, and Jesus spoke often of it. The apostle Paul required faithfulness of himself and those who ministered with him. And Timothy, Paul's co-laborer and mentee, exemplified faithfulness. Take a moment now and ask God to assist you in being faithful in all things in your everyday life. No matter whether something is big or small, whether it is serving in the church or doing quiet deeds at home, minister faithfully.

Faithfulness is a wonderful quality! May your devotion to God be evident in all you say and do so God's life in you cannot be missed.

Lord, are my words uplifting to others? Are my actions honorable and selfless? Please help me devote each of my days to You—my Father, my King, and my Lord. Amen.

Out with the Bad

Beloved, it's never too late to grow in the Lord. It's also never too late to discard behaviors that are unlike our God. And it's never too late to embrace the spiritual truths found in God's Word. Discarding the bad and desiring the good can be actions you take every day of your life. Even believers of 10, 20, or 30 years still crave the Word of God. In fact, the more you grow in Christ, the more your desire for the Word increases! Oh, how I hope and pray this is true of you!

I used to struggle with gossiping. But through consistent prayer, accountability, and the desire to be like Christ, I was finally able to eliminate gossip from my life. I encourage you to purge whatever is not righteous and good in your life too.

Lord, with Your strength, I'm ready to purge gossip and other negative uses of my voice from my life. I'm ready to discard ungodly behaviors and replace them with the truth of Your Word. Help me, Lord, to grow in You every day. Amen.

The Best Role

No role brings greater joy or blessing than being a parent. It is with love and a prayer for you that I share these principles that guided me during those active, hands-on, child-raising years:

- love your husband
- love your children
- trust God for His strength
- stand firm
- own your responsibility
- seek your husband's input
- seek wise counsel from those who have gone before you
- seek the Lord's wisdom through prayer and His Word

Lord, lead me to a deeper love and more patient understanding for my family. As I study Your Word, guide me to be wise in my parenting. Help me follow Your design to be a worthy example to my family. Amen.

Living with Passion and Purpose

Christians love to sing about following Jesus. But following Jesus is no easy task or light commitment. Jesus is a loving but demanding Master, and He expects His followers to listen, learn, and obey. Unfortunately, when Jesus taught about being the bread of life, many fairweather followers left. They simply could not accept His teaching (John 6:48-66).

Are you one who hesitates, stops, and waits? Or do you say along with Peter, "Lord, to whom shall we go? You have the words of eternal life" (John 6:68). To live with passion and purpose, you must follow Jesus wholeheartedly.

Do you know someone who needs to hear about Jesus? Be prayerful as you make plans to share the good news of the gospel.

Lord, You have called me, and I'm ready to follow.
Help me be a witness of faith and passion as I
share You with the people around me. Amen.

Game Plan of Grace

The Christian life is a battle—a *spiritual* battle. We may not like it, and we may wish otherwise, but it's true. Therefore we must fight the good fight. We must cling to two inseparable, valuable dispositions of the heart—faith and a good conscience.

Is the Holy Spirit sounding any warning to your conscience about some aspect of your behavior? Are you doing what you know is right in every area of your life? Or are you deliberately ignoring an inner tug? Take some time to reflect on these tough but important questions. Huddle with God and ask Him for the game plan. Heed His wisdom and instruction. When you fumble or drop the ball (and it will happen), God has given you a way back to His plan: "If we confess our sins, He is faithful and just to forgive us our sins and to cleanse us from all unrighteousness" (1 John 1:9).

Accept God's forgiveness and grace…and get back into the game.

> *Lord, You know I need Your guidance and*
> *instruction daily. I confess my sins to You today*
> *so that I can continue in Your plan. Please lead*
> *me through the battle to victory. Amen.*

Blessings from Heaven

Speaking from my own heart, it's been a wonderful experience becoming better acquainted with some of the many and marvelous blessings that are ours in Christ Jesus...blessings from the very heights of heaven. It's incredible to realize that as children and daughters of the King, you and I have received "every spiritual blessing" (Ephesians 1:3). Believe it, because God says it! This fact alone should prompt us to fall to our knees in adoring praise.

My friend, as you are obedient to God and rely on the power of the Spirit, you will experience the daily reality of your heavenly blessings in Christ.

Lord, help me to think of others and to share
Your love with them so they, too, can experience
the countless blessings You give. I want to hold
tightly to Your magnificent promises and the great
gifts of Your peace, love, and grace. Amen.

The Lord Is Good

It's wonderful to think about God's grace and peace. They are two of the loveliest gifts He bestows on us, and these very words move our souls.

Grace is active and means "favor"—meaning that whatever your situation is or whatever the occasion is, you have God's favor. You have all that you need to endure, cope, and have victory in any and every circumstance.

Peace, on the other hand, is passive and refers to rest. And so, my friend, whatever your situation, whatever the occasion or need, you have God's peace.

As we put on God's gentle and quiet spirit and rely on the Lord instead of our human efforts and emotions, then indeed we have much to show in the end. As the psalmist declared, "Oh, taste and see that the LORD is good; blessed is the man [or woman] who trusts in Him!" (Psalm 34:8).

> *God, I am crying out to You during a time of great strife. Thank You that Your grace and peace lead me toward adopting a gentle and quiet spirit even now...especially now. I will trust in Your strength and not my own as I wait for Your healing and direction. Amen.*

Purpose and Privilege

Do you know what your purpose is? Could you boldly declare "For this I was born" and know what the "this" is? Jesus could! He clearly stated, "For this cause I was born" when He was questioned by Pilate (John 18:37). Jesus went on to say, "I have come into the world, that I should bear witness to the truth. Everyone who is of the truth hears My voice."

Are you living out your purpose for God's good pleasure without murmuring and disputing? Are you studying God's instructions and being obedient so you can discover your great purpose in Christ? You have been given the gift of being a child of God. Your heavenly Father wants to see you shine for Him. For this cause...for this privilege...you were born to shine as lights in the world.

Father, what a gift You have given to me, Your child. Your Word is filled with Your instructions and guidance. You have also blessed me with spiritual parents like the apostle Paul, who encourages and inspires me to faithfully obey and model a heart committed to sacrifice and service. Thank You, Father. Amen.

Reason for Being

Having a purpose—a goal—is one of the most dynamic forces in human nature. With purpose a man or woman can accomplish amazing feats, achieve challenging goals, and persist through staggering difficulties.

Do you know your reason for being? And do you know the course of your day at each fresh sunrise? Joshua knew his purpose and declared, "As for me and my house, we will serve the LORD" (Joshua 24:15). Mary, the mother of Jesus, also knew her purpose. She said, "Behold the maidservant of the Lord! Let it be to me according to your word" (Luke 1:38). Paul, too, knew his purpose. He proclaimed, "For to me, to live is Christ" (Philippians 1:21). If you are unsure of your purpose, ask God and others to help you understand. Then focus on living for Christ and doing what He wants you to do.

> *God, I come before Your throne knowing that*
> *in this life I have a purpose that comes from*
> *You. Help me know how to walk in that*
> *purpose day by day. Thank You for blessing*
> *me with a reason for being. Amen.*

Pursue Godliness

Do you yearn to live a godly life…a holy life? One vital step you can take is increasing your knowledge and understanding of God's Word. Psalm 19:7-9 notes—

> The law of the LORD is perfect, converting the soul;
>
> The testimony of the LORD is sure, making wise the simple;
>
> The statutes of the LORD are right, rejoicing the heart;
>
> The commandment of the LORD is pure, enlightening the eyes;
>
> The fear of the LORD is clean, enduring forever;
>
> The judgments of the LORD are true and righteous altogether.

In Ephesians 4:29, Paul instructs us to "let no corrupt word proceed out of your mouth, but what is good for necessary edification, that it may impart grace to the hearers." In all you do and say, pursue godliness and trust God's every word.

Lord, may my words be wholesome and profitable.
May I hold tightly to the words of Jesus as truth
so that I never teach false doctrines. I want to
communicate Your truth and Your way. Amen.

You Are Never Defenseless

There are plenty of battles in our day-to-day physical lives. For example, there is the battle of the bulge, the battle with children to get them to eat vegetables, the battle to pay the bills…and the list goes on! But the one battle we most need to recognize and prepare for is the spiritual battle.

Turning to the truth of God's Word, we can become spiritually prepared to fight and win the war. War sounds intimidating, doesn't it? But God does not leave us defenseless! We can rest fully in the strength of the Lord, the power of His might, and His victory.

Ask God to give you the resolve to "take up the whole armor of God, that you may be able to withstand in the evil day, and having done all, to stand" (Ephesians 6:13). When you are victorious on this front, the battles you experience at home, at work, and in relationships are put into perspective and often resolved.

Father, I often forget to be on guard against the spiritual battle. Give me Your wisdom as I prepare for battle and Your strength and might so I can be victorious and glorify You. Amen.

Sower of Peace

We can tell a lot about a woman's faith by how well she sows wisdom and peace. In fact, there is beautiful evidence of a life that is grounded in spiritual wisdom. The Bible shows us a life that is pure, peaceable, gentle, willing to yield, full of mercy, full of good fruits, without partiality, and without hypocrisy (James 3:17). How did you do with this checklist? Are these "good fruits" evident in your life? Think about your relationships and your effect on others. Are you a promoter of peace and righteousness?

May your heart be a heart of wisdom! And may your words be filled with God's wisdom. Become the sower of peace in your family, your home, and your church. Speak words of mercy and be sincere in your forgiveness of others. You will experience the gracious beauty of a life overflowing with true wisdom—God's wisdom.

God, when I rely on my wisdom and the influences of the world, I end up sowing discontent and jealousy. Help me to bear the fruit of Your wisdom so I can bring blessings to others and praise to Your name. Amen.

God's Redeeming Love

In the quiet of spending time in God's Word, ask yourself, *Am I continuing to turn my back on my former life? Have I soberly acknowledged that God is the Judge who will judge me according to my deeds? Am I living my life in a healthy reverential fear, not as one who is afraid of God, but as one who respects and reveres and loves the all-powerful Creator?*

I know you don't want to offend God or take Him for granted. So keep checking your attitudes and behaviors. As great as the depth of your sinfulness is, that is the height of God's redeeming love. Live daily with this fact in mind…and revel in the overwhelming love for Jesus in your heart.

> *Lord, I'm so thankful for the gift of salvation and for Your presence in my life every day. I want my daily life to reflect Your presence and my gratitude to You. Keep me from returning to the ways of my past. I want my intentions and actions to always be pleasing in Your sight. Amen.*

A Humble Heart

While we may desire the exquisite grace of humility, how is such beauty realized? How can we nurture a heart of humility? Here are a few scriptural guidelines.

- *Know yourself.* We are made in the image of God, but we are also sinners in need of a renewed mind so we will think properly about ourselves.

- *Respect others.* Jesus told His disciples to major on service to others. He "did not come to be served, but to serve, and to give His life a ransom for many" (Mark 10:45).

- *Pray faithfully.* In prayer we bow humbly before God Almighty, confess our sins, praise our heavenly Father for all He has done for us, and ask for His mercy on us and on others.

- *Imitate Christ's humility.* This, my friend, is the key to lowliness of mind.

Turn your mind to Christ's sacrifice. Then turn your attention to the needs of others and minister with a humble, grateful heart.

Lord, I bow before You with a humble heart and spirit. Lead me so I will see the needs of those around me and actively serve the body of Christ. Amen.

The Grace of Giving

What do you require for contentment? Are food and clothing and shelter enough? Do you desire more than is needed when you shop? Thank God for His abundant provision for your necessities...your *true* necessities.

The Proverbs 31 woman reveals a godly balance in the area of money. Her motives were *pure*—she desired to help and to better her family. And her motives were *godly*—she gave her money to the poor and needy and assisted her community.

The best way to guard against the love of money is to be a "generous soul" (Proverbs 11:25). Who needs your money today? What missionary ministry could be bettered by your contribution? How could your church benefit from your support? Why not help the poor and needy in your community? Ask God to guide you with His beautiful grace of giving.

> *Lord, help me become a generous giver to Your church and to Your children near and far. Protect me from the love of money. I will rest in my value in You. Thank You for giving me contentment. Amen.*

Live God's Way

If you have read the four Gospels in the New Testament, you know of Jesus' famous Sermon on the Mount. In fact, some have asked, "Are the teachings of Jesus in Luke 6:20-49 part of that well-loved sermon?" While Luke's presentation contains similarities to the full sermon that was recorded in Matthew, chapters 5 through 7, it is also possible that, like all good teachers, Jesus may have given similar teachings on various occasions.

However, whether Luke's information was part of the better-known sermon or not, the important thing is that the apostles were the recipients of Jesus' teaching. They needed to grasp their purpose so that one day, when the time was right, their passion for Jesus would thrust them into a fearless ministry of boldly proclaiming the good news of the risen Savior. Are you ready to live God's way? Faithfully pray for God's vision and priorities for your life today. Then live it!

Lord, I love Your ways. I walk in them with a heart of gratitude. I pray that the fruit of my life will show others my passion for Your truth and purpose. Amen.

Marriage by Design

Marriage is often described as the union of two selfish sinners…and therein lies the problem! God did not intend for the marriage relationship to be like this. The fall of man into sin affected everything, including marriage. That's a true picture of paradise lost. But God has provided a solution for struggles in marriage, and that is Jesus Christ. Ah, paradise regained!

You can love your husband and serve your marriage when you use the biblical pattern of submission and respect. The next time your sin nature tugs at you to disrespect your husband, think of your Lord. Jesus *willingly* submitted to the Father's will because of His love for the Father. God asks you to respect and submit to your husband out of love and respect for Him. Obey God's plan and follow Christ's example. When you do this, you will be following God's perfect design for your marriage.

> *Lord, help me line up under Your command*
> *so my marriage can be all that You designed*
> *it to be. Thank You, Jesus, for giving me Your*
> *example of love and respect so I can enjoy the*
> *goodness of a healthy relationship. Amen.*

Life-Changing Love

It's easy to see that the kind of love God calls us to exhibit—sincere, fervent, and hearty—will cost us greatly and require much effort, isn't it? It may even include suffering. And if that happens, we're to put on God's gentle and quiet spirit to endure any ill treatment and still give love in return. Remember that a gentle spirit doesn't cause disturbances…and doesn't react to the disturbances caused by others. Instead we love—earnestly, genuinely, and wholeheartedly—even those who cause us to suffer.

We are to "love one another fervently with a pure heart" (1 Peter 1:22). This can be challenging, but it is also life-changing. You can do it! Extend the love God gives to you to others. It's easy to talk about how much you love God, but loving others reveals how much you truly do. It's a supernatural display of God in you. Where love resides, God abides.

> *God, give me Your heart for others*
> *so that I love others with a sincere,*
> *fervent, and hearty love. Amen.*

What's Next, Lord?

There are two conditions we should be careful not to violate in our decision-making and planning. The first is failing to consider our finiteness as humans. Let's face it—our knowledge is limited. We have no way of knowing what the future holds for us. The second is failing to consider the uncertainty of life, which James describes as a vapor (James 4:14).

What is the pattern of your life? When you discover new counsel from the Lord, do you leap immediately into action, making your new knowledge about God's will part of your life? Or do you wait, hanging on to a few favorite sins, before you relinquish them and do the right thing?

Being a good steward of your time is important. You don't know what the future holds, but you do know the One who holds the future! Ask God, "What's next?"

God, You are the only One who knows what tomorrow will bring. As I take steps forward to make the most of each day, guide me and remind me to be open to any unexpected turns You might bring my way. Amen.

A Prayer for Us

And this I pray, dear friend and sister in Christ, for you and me:

I pray that we learn the discipline of lifting our thoughts, prayers, and lives heavenward.

I pray that we become strong women of prayer with regular, unhurried, secret lingering in prayer.

I pray that others will be encouraged by knowing we pray for them.

I pray we will use Paul's wisdom found in Philippians 1:9-11 as our guide to praying for others.

> This I pray, that your love may abound still more and more in knowledge and all discernment, that you may approve the things that are excellent, that you may be sincere and without offense till the day of Christ, being filled with the fruits of righteousness which *are* by Jesus Christ, to the glory and praise of God.

I pray that we will live lives that bring glory to our Lord and be filled with the fruits of righteousness.

God, give me a vision for those things that are eternal and of spiritual importance. Also help me be sincere and faithful when I pray for others. Amen.

Keep Watch

Do you want to learn and grow so you can better understand the doctrines of the Christian faith and teach them to your children and help others? You can start by studying the Bible, attending church and Bible classes, and memorizing Scripture. The more you know, the more effective your protection of your loved ones will be. How can you keep from being fooled by false teaching? The answer: by being familiar with the truth! Put W-A-T-C-H to work in your life today:

Want to be with God's people

Ask God for discernment

Take in God's Word

Carefully select a Bible-teaching church

Heed the warnings of Scripture

Always keep watch over your spiritual well-being so you can help your family and friends distinguish light from dark.

Lord, my attention so easily gets caught up in daily needs and tasks. Paul reminds me to pay attention to the influences around my family and me. Give me a heart of discernment so I can watch out for those who do not teach Your truths. Amen.

Walk in Wisdom

God's ultimate wisdom and plan for you is to "be filled with the Spirit" (Ephesians 5:18). Here Paul is not referring to the Holy Spirit's indwelling at salvation. He is giving a command for believers to live continually under the influence of the Holy Spirit. He is charging you and all believers to walk in wisdom as you live moment-by-moment under the control and guidance of the Holy Spirit. What a difference that will make in your heart, in your conduct, in your priorities, and in the ways you choose to use your time!

As you are guided by the Holy Spirit, tell the Lord you want to:

- know Him better
- look with great hope to His upward calling
- understand your special relationship as His heir
- experience His power in your life

Every day you have access to God's presence, plan, and wisdom. Praise Him!

Lord, I'm practicing Your wisdom and discovering the joys of being obedient and faithful! I no longer lean on the world's offering of what is best or right. I know the truth because it is in Your Word and in my heart. Amen.

Honorable Work

Whether we work for an individual or a company, we need to obey the directives of our employers. But if we are asked to violate God's Word, we have the freedom to say "no" and change jobs. There is…

- a right way to respond to our bosses and supervisors—to submit
- a right motive for submission—praise from God
- a right attitude toward those "over" us—respect
- a right reason for suffering for doing good—becoming like Jesus
- a right manner for enduring suffering—patiently

These "rights" rule out a lot of wrongs, including rebellion, anger, a bad attitude, hostility, ambition, disdain, discontent, pride, gossip, undermining, shirking, lip service, and revenge. And I'm sure you can add to the list!

Lord, I work hard to be successful and please my employer. But most of all, I want my work and effort to honor You. Help me see when my attitude is negative and when I need to change. Most of all I pray that following Your instructions will ultimately lead people to You. Amen.

Aspire to Faithfulness

Faithfulness is a high calling because you and I want to be faithful so we can please and honor our Lord Jesus. We don't look for recognition, but we will do well in our arenas of service. Faithfulness is not one heroic act. Instead, it's an everyday kind of commitment to service. So let's quietly—and faithfully—go about the everyday business of serving others in our roles as wives, mothers, daughters, aunts, mentors, and women of God.

In what areas of your life do you want to aspire to greater service and faithfulness? Do you depend on God's strength as you fulfill the vital responsibilities He has given to you? Your godliness will benefit others and be a beacon of light in a dark world. And it will yield rich rewards for you.

God, I will strive to be faithful and to serve in
Your name with honor and integrity. May I
be one of Your lights in this world. Amen.

Time to Prepare

Even the most patient of us rarely likes to wait very long. But when we consider that our time of waiting is also a time of preparation, that changes our outlook. When John the Baptist baptized Jesus, it was God's perfect timing for Jesus' preparation to be turned into ministry action.

Unfortunately, many Christians fail to prepare to minister to the body of Christ. To live with passion and purpose means we are aggressively taking advantage of each day to help others gear up for greater things. We are spending time in preparation so we will be ready when more opportunities to serve the Lord come our way.

Are you preparing for ministry today? Are you actively helping others? What can you do to continue preparing for more service to the Lord and those around you?

Lord, I pray each day to be walking in Your will.
Help me discover ways I can prepare so I can be
of more service to You and Your people. Guide
me, lead me…and I will gladly follow! Amen.

Your Story of Peace

Jim and I have some incredible neighbors—a husband and wife who both serve their country through military service. In recent years, one was deployed to Iraq and the other to Afghanistan with the goal of bringing peace to those countries. When their tours of duty were complete, instead of coming home, their units remained deployed because the goal of peace had not yet been achieved. Peace is still not a reality.

History reveals that most human peace missions fail. But the peace achieved by the blood of Christ is real and eternal. I hope you have grasped the peace our Savior accomplished between you and God, and between you and all believers. We are all in the Lord's embrace.

What is your story of peace? What wells up in your heart and soul when you recall the moment the barrier between you and God was removed?

> *Lord, You removed the barriers that divided me*
> *from You and from others who believe in You.*
> *Thank You for giving me a clear path to peace*
> *through You. You, Lord, are my light. Amen.*

49

Peace Be with You

Two kinds of peace are given to us through God: *interpersonal peace* and *personal peace.* Unfortunately, everyone has been in situations of strife with others. Instead of giving in to your emotions, thank God for the ability to promote the interpersonal peace available through His Holy Spirit! Personal peace is needed when we face difficulties and sorrows. When your peace is interrupted,

- release your tendency to *panic*…and instead rest in God's *presence*
- release your tendency to *tremble*…and instead depend on God's *truth*
- release your tendency to *dread*…and instead accept God's *dealings*

Peter was with the Lord when He said, "Peace I leave with you, My peace I give to you; not as the world gives do I give to you. Let not your heart be troubled, neither let it be afraid" (John 14:27). This incredible peace is for you, dear sister.

> *Lord, thank You for Your peace. During times of turmoil with others or trials that are heavy on my heart, Your peace is sufficient and always present. Amen.*

It's a Given

I remember telling a group of women that my husband, Jim, and I didn't pray about taking care of our parents. That's because it was a "given." The Scripture says to care for them, so that's what we planned to do. That's when I noticed the shock on their faces. We had quite a discussion. But there it is in the Bible: "If anyone does not provide for his own, and especially for those of his household, he has denied the faith and is worse than an unbeliever" (1 Timothy 5:8).

As hard as it was to care for all of our parents through their declining years, we have no regrets. One thing that a woman who loves God does is care for her family members. Yes, it takes time, money, and effort. But it's also good and acceptable in the sight of God.

Lord, give me eyes to see the needs present in my own family. God, You promised to care for the widow, the orphan, and those who call on Your name. May I serve You by serving them faithfully. Amen.

Dress for Spiritual Success

Have you struggled to rest in the Bible's truths? To stand for God? To follow Christ faithfully? Well, take heart! You are not alone. These battles are part of a great spiritual war involving this world…and the entire universe. Praise God, the ultimate victory has been won by Christ! What can you do to ensure you are strong and will be victorious in your stand against Satan?

- put on truth
- put on the breastplate of righteousness
- put on the gospel of peace
- pick up the shield of faith
- put on the helmet of salvation
- wield the sword of the Spirit

Dressing for spiritual success is a head-to-toe process. Be sure you are putting on and wearing this armor so you can win the daily struggles of living for Christ wholeheartedly.

Lord, I will follow You into spiritual battle
dressed for victory. May I never take for
granted my faith. Remind me to use it as my
shield each day. Guide me with Your strength.
Each victory is to Your glory. Amen.

Count It Joy

How can we deal with trials? The Bible says, "Count it all joy when you fall into various trials, knowing that the testing of your faith produces patience" (James 1:2-3). Joy? Yes, joy is possible, and here's how:

By the use of your mind. No matter how you feel, choose to count your situation joy! You will reap the blessings of joy, patience, and completion as you look forward to the outcome to greater spiritual maturity and stronger faith.

By the use of your faith. Choose to look at each trial with faith to see the hand of God. When you suffer, choose to *believe* in the goodness of God and in His perfecting process of you and your faith. Believe during the painful times that God loves you and is in perfect control. And believe in the positive results of your testing—a closer relationship with your heavenly Father.

Lord, help me live in faith and believe in Your plan, Your love, and Your purpose during my trials. I choose to walk forward in this situation with a prayerful heart and an eye on the future. Amen.

Time with Jesus

Martha and Mary were extremely fortunate because they were able to be with Jesus while He was living in bodily form on this earth. In the account found in Luke 10, the two sisters provided Jesus with a good meal and sat in His physical presence, talking and asking questions.

Although we don't understand everything that is happening around us, we do have Jesus living in us as a constant presence in our lives! For instance,

- we can focus on Him
- we can reach out in His name to someone in need of compassion
- we can serve a meal to someone who needs food or hospitality
- we can have ongoing dialogue with Jesus through prayer

Think about it: We are so blessed to have time with Jesus! Through the presence of our Sustainer, we can take the strength and compassion we draw from Him to serve Him and to share Him with those in our world.

Lord, I want to sit at Your feet as Your disciple and friend. Help me turn my heart toward You and toward Your will. Amen.

A Faithful Woman

Let's purpose to never miss an opportunity to do something useful, to better the lives of others, and to do something of eternal value. There are three qualities I encourage you to develop that will help you, whether you are married, single, widowed, young, or old. A faithful woman has...

- *Self-control.* Any woman can give in to sensuality and dishonor the name of Christ. Keep these behaviors in check and remain pure as a woman of God.

- *Servant behavior.* Bad habits are most often produced by idleness. If we take precious time away from our families and our service to God by watching too much television, talking too much on the phone, and spending too much time skimming the Internet, we will become busybodies instead of busy servants.

- *Faithfulness.* A commitment to marriage and family fills our hearts and creates in us an even greater desire to honor Christ and serve those in our homes and our communities.

Lord, when I'm tempted to fill my time with
worldly pleasures and useless activities, help me to
remain faithful. I desire to live above reproach.
I want to be beautiful in and for You. Amen.

Grace and Peace Are Yours

We are so fortunate to be God's women! The twin resources of God's grace and God's peace are ours:

- *God's grace* is His unmerited favor poured out upon those who have trusted in Jesus Christ. Just as God is all we need, so God's grace covers everything we can think of and more.

- *God's peace* is ours when we approach Him with childlike confidence and trust and hope. Truly we have peace with God, the peace of God, and the God of peace. We have all that we need for total well-being.

What is your most pressing trial or difficulty today? Identify it and tap into these two supernatural resources— God's grace and God's peace. They are available and all yours if you belong to the family of God through Jesus Christ.

> *Lord, I want to be Your slave. With the power and might of Your grace and peace, help me live a life that pleases You. Give me the heart of a faithful servant, and remind me that You are the perfect Master. Amen.*

What Really Matters

I am sure you face many of the challenges I face—personal problems, worries, anxieties, temptations, disappointments, and more. Studies have shown that when a greater anxiety or concern comes along, the lesser ones fade away. What does this mean? It means if you want to be free of your worries and anxieties, then you must lose yourself in the real issues of life like:

- the relationships that really matter
- the issues that are close to your heart
- the spiritual battles you and others face
- the second coming of Jesus
- whether people have chosen God through Jesus or not

And then pray! When you do, you will discover that it is almost impossible to worry about yourself and pray for others at the same time. And don't forget to pray for yourself. You want to be strong in the power of God's might and reach out to others with the good news of the gospel.

*God, when I focus on the real matters of my
life instead of anticipating problems, I am
better able to help the needs of those around
me. Remind me to bring my needs and those
of others to You for daily prayer. Amen.*

Never Alone

Have you ever had the privilege of looking at a painted picture of the body of our Lord Jesus Christ? I thank God for Peter, the verbal artist who has used superb imagery to paint a picture of the body of Christ. It is both comforting and humbling. In 1 Peter 2:6, Peter tells us, "Behold, I lay in Zion a chief cornerstone, elect, precious, and he who believes on Him will by no means be put to shame." You are building your eternal life on the chief cornerstone (Jesus) and are supported by other "living stones" when you fellowship with other believers.

There is nothing we will have to do or bear alone. We are part of a "spiritual house"—the church of God. Its foundation is Christ, and it possesses strength and beauty based on a wide variety of materials...including you! It is a comfort and privilege to be a part of the Lord's house and the big picture of the body of Christ. You are truly never alone.

God, I have felt alone. I have also tried to live my life without support, without leaning on You as my cornerstone. Thank You for reminding me that I am always with other believers in Your magnificent house. Amen.

Pause and Pray

Isn't it amazing that all we have to do is ask God for guidance with a heart full of faith…and wisdom will be given to us? Whenever you face your trials or dilemmas, instead of praying for the removal of your test, ask God to give you the wisdom you need to handle your trials His way. Stop, look, and listen before you move ahead:

- *Stop* before you do anything. This gives you time to consult the Lord before you act.
- *Look* to the Lord. Boldly ask, "Lord, what do You want me to do here?"
- *Listen* for His wisdom. A heart of faith believes God hears your cry for help…and He answers.
- *Respond* to Him in obedience without doubt.
- *Proceed* because you know God's wisdom is best.

These actions and attitudes of faith make up the secret to wisdom. You will face trial after trial, but you now know *how* to face them!

> *Lord, today I am asking for Your guidance.*
> *Please help me discover the secret to wisdom*
> *so I can discern Your Word and Your will as*
> *I grow and move forward in You. Amen.*

Don't Give Up

As we think about living with passion and purpose, we can look to Jesus who remained passionate about His message, especially as He moved toward the cross. Sadly, Jesus' sermon on hypocrisy further inflamed the fear and hatred of the religious leaders toward Him. Yet His message is loud and clear: All must get right with God! Judgment is coming, and by immersing ourselves in God's passionate instruction and love, you and I are becoming whole through His salvation and grace.

Are you facing opposition to your faith? Ask God to help you stand firm in Him. And what about the coming judgment? Ask God to give you His love and boldness to speak of Jesus' return, even to those who are hostile. Don't give up on others. Jesus didn't.

God, grant me discernment and a convicted heart so I will come clean and unveil all my sins to You. Help me to live a life that will hold up under scrutiny, a life that receives Your grace and healing and serves You wholeheartedly. Amen.

Abundant Grace

Have you ever had a Wow Day? Well, I'm having one right now. Wow! My heart is overflowing with gratitude to God and Christ Jesus. As Paul put it, "The grace of our Lord was exceedingly abundant, with faith and love which are in Christ Jesus" (1 Timothy 1:14). Paul is telling us that God's grace is "super abundant" and way more than adequate for all our sins.

Why not do as Paul did? Why not make his response your response? Give thanks to God for His mercy. Burst forth in a doxology—praising and expressing glory to God! Spend time now in an outpouring of praise and glory to God. You may also want to write it out. And why not share it with others?

Lord, thank You for Your sweet mercy. It has
covered my sinful past and provided me with
a new journey that ends in eternity with You.
May my life be an example of Your saving
grace and my deep gratitude. Amen.

In All Circumstances

No matter where you start, and no matter the condition of the port that you are leaving, as a believer you can apply God's message to your personal situation and to all circumstances with absolute faith. For instance...

- *The lowly.* If you live on meager means, you are to rejoice in the fact that you are a child of God and a joint heir with Christ (Romans 8:16-17).

- *The rich.* If you have wealth, James 1:9-11 essentially says, "Be sure you put no store in your riches. Life is uncertain. As quickly as the newly risen sun wilts and withers the grass, so your riches can disappear. Don't place your trust in external things you can lose in a second. Trust instead in the Lord and in His eternal riches."

One thing is for sure: The ground at the foot of the cross is level. Trials are the great equalizer, leveling all believers in all circumstances to dependence on God.

> *Lord, in the trial I am facing I am going to*
> *set sail. In all my circumstances I am going*
> *to trust You, Lord, and rely on Your promises*
> *to navigate, keep me safe, and provide the*
> *wisdom I need to reach the other side. Amen.*

The Habit of Praise

As a believer in Jesus Christ and one who trusts in Him, you have been given an inheritance in Him that is sealed and guaranteed by the Holy Spirit. But you were not saved and blessed for your own glory. No, it was for *God's* glory. Your redemption becomes an example of God's great grace for others. When others see how God moves in your life, they will want to know God and also be led by Him. Isn't it incredible that God allows you to assist Him in such a personal and lasting way?

Give God your heart response of praise for your salvation. And make it your habit to praise Him daily. This is one thing you can do on earth that you will continue to do in heaven.

> *Lord, I am so grateful to receive Your heavenly*
> *inheritance. I can now walk through my days*
> *with a heart full of praise and thanksgiving.*
> *May my life reflect how grateful I am for the*
> *blessings You have given to me…and continue*
> *to give me. Thank You! I praise You for my*
> *hope, my future, and my faith in You. Amen.*

Living and Dying for Christ

Paul, God's suffering servant, shows us how to live, and he also shows us how to die: "For to me, to live is Christ, and to die is gain" (Philippians 1:21). Paul yearned to be with the Lord he loved, yet he knew that each day he lived was another day to serve Christ. What a wonderful example for you and me!

Life is more than planning for retirement, saving money, purchasing a recreational vehicle, traveling, and living it up. Life is about living for and in Christ every day that you are able. It's about looking ahead with hope and longing for that day when you will be in the presence of the Lord forever.

Make Philippians 1:21 your creed for life and death, and keep heaven in view as you serve the Lord each day.

Lord, I want each day to count for Your glory.
Please give me strength to be a strong witness
of You to others. I long to live abundantly in
You on this earth and then be in heaven with
You. I want to remember along with Paul that
"to live is Christ, and to die is gain." Amen.

Our Why and Our Who

I have an easier time doing something that doesn't come naturally when I know *why* it needs to be done. How about you? This is also true with submission. God tells us to "submit," but He also clearly tells us why: We are to "submit [ourselves] for the Lord's sake" (1 Peter 2:13 NIV). Could any answer to the question *why* be bigger or matter more?

The *why* of our submission is wrapped up in the *who* of our submission—God. He is asking us to submit for His sake. It is His will. So, He's asking us to serve Him in our submission to others.

And here's another thought: *God is sovereign.* He knows all about the existing governments and officials and what He is accomplishing through them. Discover the comfort and power of simply trusting the Lord.

As servants of God, and knowing it is His will and for His sake, submit.

Lord, help me have a willing spirit and a
servant's heart as I accept Your authority and put
submission into practice in my daily life. Amen.

Stay Encouraged and Faithful

My friend, does your faith compel you to follow Christ's example and to become an example of Him? Press on in these ways:

- *Follow Christians.* Spend time with someone in your life who shows you how to follow in Christ's footsteps. If you are new to the faith, ask God to lead you to someone who is looking to the Lord and following hard after Him (Psalm 63:8).

- *Model Jesus.* Be one who models for others what it means to be a true follower of Jesus. I pray that you will be able to say along with Paul, "Imitate me, just as I also imitate Christ" (1 Corinthians 11:1).

- *Remain alert and prayerful.* Be sure you follow those who follow the Lord and are not enemies of Jesus. Always seek God's wisdom as you follow Christ and build up those who seek to do the same.

> God, I want to keep my eyes on You and my heart focused on Your Word. I will look to those who follow You for guidance. I am "a friend of the cross" and want to lead others to You. Please help me do that. Amen.

Look Upward

P aul's focus on eternity is a magnificent example for us. What can we learn from him?

> Keep this commandment...until our Lord Jesus Christ's appearing, which He will manifest in His own time, He who is the blessed and only Potentate, the King of kings and Lord of lords, who alone has immortality, dwelling in unapproachable light, whom no man has seen or can see, to whom be honor and everlasting power (1 Timothy 6:14-16).

In the midst of fighting his own fight for the faith, Paul's focus is not on temporal things but is set on godliness, on eternal life, on the fact of God's presence, on Jesus Christ, and on His second coming.

Where are your sights set, my friend? As a woman of God, you are to "seek those things which are above" and "set your mind on things above" (Colossians 3:1-2). Let's look upward together!

> *God, I am looking upward and keeping my eyes*
> *on my victory in You. Prepare me and instruct*
> *me so I can keep my eyes on You. Amen.*

Prayer Is the Beginning

Through selfless prayer, you can give all of your areas of strife and conflict to God. When the inside of your heart is free of selfish desire, you will not crave combat and deception. Instead, you will hunger for God's peace.

Do you know there is a "wrong way" to pray? One wrong way is to not pray at all. Another wrong way to pray is to ask for things related to lustful desires or selfish wants instead of what will further God's will and purposes for you. One more wrong way to pray is to ask for the wrong things and for the wrong reasons. For instance, do you want to impress someone, or are you sincerely seeking to benefit God and His plan?

Lift your motives before the Lord. Acknowledge any sinful thoughts and adjust them to match God's good and perfect will. Truly, prayer is the beginning of the solution to the problem of strife.

Lord, examine my heart. Reveal the strife and selfish desires that work against my quest for Your peace. Help me get rid of those attitudes and remember that prayer each day is the beginning of all good things. Amen.

A Daily Choice

Have you ever considered that every day you are choosing to be *either* an enemy toward the world *or* an enemy toward God? Search your heart and consider the kinds of choices you have made during the past hour…week…year. Are you building a friendship with God or with the world?

God longs to see His Spirit evidenced in your life. When you are humbly seeking to live wholly for Him, you will receive the gracious help you need to do just that. God blesses the humble-minded and favors the lowly with His continual grace for continual growth. Pray for ways you can humbly seek a life that pleases God, and ask for the assistance of His great and marvelous grace.

When you make it a daily choice to turn your eyes to Jesus, you won't be interested in the trinkets the world offers. You will be consumed with *Him*—the light of His glory and grace. Turn your eyes to Jesus today.

> *Lord, I am learning to make a daily choice
> to fix my eyes on You. Help me see where and
> how I have been flirting with the world. I
> want to turn my thoughts and attention and
> actions toward eternity with You. Amen.*

Standing Firm in the Struggle

Strong faith stands up well in persecution. It also withstands the pressure of trials. Just as an athlete strengthens his or her muscles through the discipline of a regular regimen, so you and I can nurture a stronger faith that will enable us to conduct ourselves in a way that is worthy of Christ. What do we need to do?

- read God's Word regularly
- pray for greater faith
- read biographies of Christians that will inspire our faith and perseverance

We also need to trust God during the times of refining fire. By standing firm during these struggles, our commitment to Christ will be deepened, our faith will be strengthened, our passion to live for Him will be ignited, and our conduct will be worthy. Depend on God and trust Him to bring about His good and perfect will in your trial.

> *God, when I face those who oppose my faith*
> *and speak against Your ways, give me the*
> *boldness to stand fast. Thank You for these*
> *hard times that draw me closer to You and*
> *reveal the purpose You have for me. Amen.*

Let God Hear Your Prayers

When we have a physical ailment, many times the treatment is painful. Surgery sets us back, and chemotherapy and radiation knock us down. Even stitches and injections hurt. Yet in the end we are helped and relieved. That's what the Lord wants for us. He wants to help us be rid of sin because it harms us. And sometimes the treatment hurts. It's difficult to admit mistakes, to ask for prayer, and to seek forgiveness. But in the end, we are better people.

God is calling us to walk uprightly, to admit our sin when we fail and fall. He also appeals to others to pray on our behalf, and for us to do the same for others—praying always.

Where does your life find you today? Are you suffering...or are you cheerful? Are you ill...or are you praying for someone who is? Pray constantly! Let God hear your prayers at every turn, in every situation, and for every need.

> Lord, my heart longs to be in Your presence.
> When I face pain, adversity, temptation,
> illness, worries, and times of gladness, I will
> lift up my words and my life to You. Amen.

Representing Jesus

You bear a great label—*Christian*—and you have a great responsibility to live up to it. There is a story about a soldier in Alexander the Great's army. This soldier was called up to be court-martialed for desertion. Alexander asked the man, "What is your name?" "Alexander," was the man's reply. The king then commanded, "Then change your name or change your ways."

Our conduct is an advertisement for or against Jesus Christ. That's why unity in the body of Christ is so important. Jesus prayed that His disciples and the church would live out their calling and be unified. By the sustaining power of God's Spirit, you can work toward unity in the faith.

As you live your life and build relationships with others, always remember that you are representing the label *Christian*. And most important of all, you are representing the name of Jesus Christ, the Lord.

Lord, I want to be a billboard for You in
everything I do. Help me respond to others with
grace and kindness and compassion. I want
to be worthy of my calling in You. Amen.

Invest in What Lasts

I'm sure you have discovered that success comes with a price. Well, it is no different in the Christian life. Jesus freely let people leave who were not willing to pay the price of following Him. He cautioned one person who wanted to delay following Him and said, "No one, having put his hand to the plow, and looking back, is fit for the kingdom of God" (Luke 9:62).

Being a disciple of Christ is not a one-time transaction. Jesus was asking His followers—and is asking you and me—to count the cost on a daily basis as we live for Him. Invest in those things that will last. It's not easy to pick up your cross and follow Jesus, but when you do, your purpose unfolds and your life is filled with joy and significance!

Lord, I want to follow You no matter what it costs. With Your strength and grace, I will let go of any habits, possessions, and attitudes that stand between me and Your way. Help me willingly pick up my cross and dedicate my life to You. Amen.

So Much to Pray About!

Praying God's way for the leaders of our country—whether they are hostile toward or supportive of Christianity—can make a difference in their lives, in our country, in our churches, and in our lives. Prayer changes *things*, but prayer also changes *us*.

So pray! Pray for governmental officials. Pray for those in authority. Pray for your church leadership. Pray for your friends. Pray for your enemies (Luke 6:28). And, dear woman (and wife and mother and daughter and sister and aunt), follow after God's own heart and *pray* fervently for your family. *Give thanks* for those in your family circle who love the Lord Jesus Christ. *Intercede* for your loved ones. *Commit* to impassioned *supplication* for your spouse...or child...or mother or father...or brother or sister...who doesn't embrace Jesus.

Can you see? You can pray about many things and for many people. What a joy and privilege!

> *God, it is a great blessing to be able to come to You about the people I love...and even those who persecute me. Fill my heart with love and compassion and hope as I lift up prayers of supplication, intercession, and thanksgiving. Amen.*

A Life That Counts

I could go on and on in praise of two verses found in 1 Timothy 2:9-10. These verses form what I call one of the "pink passages" of the Bible—one of the sections in God's Word that spells out for women exactly what it means to be a true woman of excellence.

Another "pink passage"—1 Timothy 5:10—shows us God's priorities, God's standard, and God's design for our everyday lives: "If she has brought up children, if she has lodged strangers, if she has washed the saints' feet, if she has relieved the afflicted, if she has diligently followed every good work." God calls us to a life of service.

In what areas do you shine? In what areas could you use some improvement? Pray about both areas and dedicate yourself to God and to service in His name. There is goodness and godliness in a life of service to others.

Lord, I want my life to count. May my mission and vision be to serve You and others and to pursue good works with passion and sincerity. Amen.

Prepared for Battle

Whether we like it or not, Christians have always been compared to soldiers, and the battle that we wage against sin and evil has been likened to war. To adequately wage the war God calls us to fight, we need God's help. We need motivation, training, discipline, and endurance. Achieving victory also demands that we be unified and vigilant. Unity is accomplished as we submit to one another, and vigilance is expressed as we resist the devil and the forces of evil.

No army ever gets a job done without the cooperation, obedience, and quick responses of its soldiers.

How do we begin the battle? "Humble yourselves under the mighty hand of God, that He may exalt you in due time, casting all your care upon Him, for He cares for you" (1 Peter 5:6-7). Our humbled and surrendered hearts prepare us to walk in the victory God has for us, no matter the battles we face.

> *God, give me a warrior's heart and strength as I begin each day ready and willing to be united, obedient, and sent into battle. With humility, I am prepared to follow where You lead me. Amen.*

A Woman of Hope

Here are a few passionate words from the apostle Paul. He wrote these uplifting lines in Romans 8:28-29: "We know that all things work together for good to those who love God, to those who are the called according to His purpose. For whom He foreknew, He also predestined to be conformed to the image of His Son." Knowing God and trusting in His promise to work all things together for good makes you and me women of hope. We can have hope because our God is in control of all things—even those things that appear to be negative.

When we choose to bloom where our all-wise God plants us, we will one day be able to declare with Paul, "I want you to know, brethren, that the things which happened to me have actually turned out for the furtherance of the gospel" (Philippians 1:12). Don't forget to declare your hope to the world.

God, help me accept where I am now and see the blessings and opportunities that are right in front of me. I trust in You to be in control of all things. May others see and know the hope I have in You. Amen.

Let Them See Your Passion

I believe a Christian woman's heart for God should be like a teakettle on a flaming stove burner—hot to the touch, visibly steaming, and audible. The heat of her love moves her to activity and her passion for Christ, the object of her affection and enthusiasm. Indeed, everyone within earshot hears about the great things He who is mighty has done for her (Luke 1:49).

What is your response to the Savior? How audible is your passion for Jesus? And how intense is the heat of your love for our Lord? The presence of the Savior should inspire a fervent reaction in your soul. Does your passion for the Son of Man show? Are you glorifying and praising God for all you know and have heard? And are others hearing of your passion for Christ?

> *God, may the truths about Christ turn my belief*
> *into action and praise. I want to share with anyone*
> *who will hear the good news of You. Amen.*

A Heart of Reverence

I'm sure you agree that as a godly woman you cannot claim to revere and worship God and at the same time disregard His plan for your behavior and your roles as a woman. From my heart to yours, here is what I and Paul and God's Word want for you and me. Stop struggling and wrangling over the issues of teaching or silence or submission in the church (1 Timothy 2:9-13). Instead, show a godly heart attitude by your ministry of good works in the church and with your family at home.

Actively striving for a reverential heart attitude will be shown in our actions and behaviors. God *will* bless us as we pursue godliness and a lovely heart attitude.

God, I want to honor You with the way I dress,
behave, and serve the church and my family. When
the world confuses me about my roles, help me return
to the focus and guidance of Your Word. Amen.

The Fruit of Your Lips

To bless or to curse? Only you can answer this choice
for your life. Did you know that the word *gossip* is
used in the Bible for the devil? His name is *diabolos*, which
means "slanderer." In fact, in the Greek Scriptures, *diabolos* is used 34 times as a title for Satan and once to refer to
Judas, who betrayed Jesus (John 6:70).

No woman who loves God wants to be a gossip or
a slanderer (literally a "she-devil"). Jesus taught that the
devil is a liar and the father of lies (John 8:44). And I'm
sure you don't want to act like the devil, the accuser of the
brethren and our adversary who "walks about like a roaring lion, seeking whom he may devour" (1 Peter 5:8).

Won't you choose to honor God and bless the people
around you with sweet fruit from your lips?

> *Lord, I can't tame my tongue, but I can bring
> my heart, my speech, my tongue, and my need
> to gossip under the control of the Holy Spirit.
> I want my speech to be a blessing. Amen.*

Be of Good Cheer

I wish it weren't true, but suffering is a fact of life. It's just as Jesus declared: "In the world you will have tribulation" (John 16:33). But aren't you glad that Jesus went on to add, "But be of good cheer, I have overcome the world"? You can experience great joy in your trials when, first, your suffering is for doing what is right, and second, when you look forward to spending time in Jesus' presence.

Friend, we have been given all things that pertain to life and to living life in a godly manner (2 Peter 1:3). And that "all things" includes the grace to endure suffering for doing what is right. When trials come your way, look to the Lord! And look to the glory and joy He promises to give His suffering children.

Lord, You know the affliction I am currently experiencing. My circumstances grieve me, but I am holding on to the knowledge of Your provision. I will press on and do the right thing in Your name. Amen.

Habit of Prayer

Take the time to memorize, pray, and live the Lord's prayer (Matthew 6:9-13). In an ungodly world, Jesus lived with fiery passion. His disciples were reminded daily of His zeal as they watched Him minister to people. Where did Jesus get His energy and enthusiasm? One answer is obvious—His habit of prayer.

Do you long for more passion in your Christian life? To be more like Jesus? Then pray. As you make prayer a habit, you will discover God's purpose for you. As you pray and choose to believe, your days will become pointed rather than pointless, full rather than empty, and vibrant rather than lifeless.

Lord, through prayer I have Your power to stand strong when there is conflict, evil, resistance, and temptation. Thank You. Amen.

Pleasing the Lord

What Christian doesn't want to please God? As Jesus said, "If you love Me, keep My commandments" (John 14:15). How can you show your love for Christ? Paul gives you the answer: "Be filled with the Spirit" (Ephesians 5:18). When you choose to walk in obedience to God's Word, you are pleasing the Lord, and His Spirit will empower you to:

- give praise out of a joyful heart
- give thanks out of a grateful heart
- give honor to others out of a submissive heart

Aren't you continually in awe that the God of the universe indwells you and gives you guidance for every action when you submit your will to Him? I am! So go to the place you know—God's presence—and embrace the joy of your salvation.

Lord, I'm filled with awe because You are faithful and all-powerful. Joy springs up in my heart today because I know Your commands and am experiencing Your love. I gladly follow You with all my heart. Amen.

Heart Checkups

Jesus, the ultimate Counselor, said, "Out of the abundance of the heart the mouth speaks" (Matthew 12:34). It's true that we speak and act out of what is in our hearts. So how about a heart checkup? Do you...

- love one another (John 13:34-35)?
- pray for one another (Ephesians 6:18)?
- respect one another (Philippians 2:3-4)?
- comfort one another (1 Thessalonians 5:11)?
- edify one another (Romans 14:19)?

How do you handle people? Do you have a tendency to strike harshly or scold with words? If you are a mom, how do you handle the "little people" in your home? I encourage you to strengthen your walk with the Lord and have regular spiritual heart checkups so your heart for others—your compassion—is refreshed.

Lord, help me have a loving heart attitude.
Give me Your wisdom and encouraging
words to share so I can help others. Amen.

Going to the Source

How do we become women of faith and exhibit faith in action? We can search for the answers in the source of all knowledge and wisdom—God's Word.

Where does faith come from? The answer is *grace*—specifically God's grace. In Ephesians 2:8-10, we learn that by grace we are saved. And that grace is a gift from God. Faith is a work of God in our hearts. Here are two surefire ways to nurture and strengthen faith:

- *Reading God's Word.* When we read the Bible, we see the trials, testing, and temptations people faced, how they faced each situation, what they did, and how it turned out.

- *Hearing God's Word.* Hearing the Bible taught and explained fuels our faith and motivates us to learn more.

Make it a point to share God's Word and back up its teachings with your works and actions.

Lord, I want my life to be a clear example of Your grace. Help me reach out to others and stand for righteousness. Guide me in Your wisdom so that I may become a woman of faith—and action! Amen.

Keep Growing

It's one thing to watch out for others, but a woman of faith must also watch out for herself. Have you heard the saying, "You're either moving forward or backward. There is no such thing as standing still in the Christian life"? What can hurt your spiritual growth more than anything? The answer: doing nothing! Passivity can and does have a disastrous effect on spiritual growth.

Another way to wander from the truth is to actively turn away from what is best. Are there any "second-best" choices you are making or have made that are leading you away from your love for Christ? How will you set your feet once again on the best path of growing?

May the *works* of your faith match the *words* of your faith. Keep growing, and may your walk align with your talk.

> Lord, please give me a heart that is sensitive to
> those who are straying from Your truth. Help me
> approach them with compassion and integrity.
> May my walk always align with my talk…and
> may both demonstrate a heart of love. Amen.

The Power of Peace

Aren't you glad that God is the Author, the Perfector, and the Finisher of all that He begins? He is omniscient and sees the end product as perfect and complete. Because God is in control of all things, including your life, He is also the power of peace in your life.

To experience the power of peace in every situation, begin with thanksgiving. Giving thanks is commanded by God. His Word tells us to give thanks *always* and for *all* things, in *everything* (1 Thessalonians 5:16-18). Once you decide to give thanks, there will be a powerful effect on your attitude and your peace. "The peace of God, which surpasses all understanding," is indeed available to you (Philippians 4:7). With this gift in your life, you will always have something to thank God for.

Lord, thank You for being the Author and
Perfecter of my faith. Help me remember
that my joy and peace are grounded in
You…and not in my circumstances. Amen.

Day-by-Day Progress

Some scriptures call for a heart response of prayer, thanksgiving, humility, and inspiration. Others call for action. I'm sure you know that when it comes to spiritual growth, you are not on autopilot. You did *not* possess right attitudes or think right thoughts or make right decisions the instant you became a child of God. No, growth into Christlikeness is a process, a day-by-day progression. It requires listening to God's Spirit as He prompts, convicts, and encourages. Glorious results are sure to follow!

If you are obedient to follow Jesus' leading, you will be continually changing from the inside—in your character, values, attitudes, perspectives, and motives. And, blessing upon blessings, these inner changes will be noticed by others who will see Jesus Christ reflected in your transformed heart.

*Lord, I'm listening for Your leading. I am embracing
the clear teachings of Your Word. Thank You for
providing it and for letting it speak so directly to
my heart. Help me step forward with integrity,
compassion, selflessness, and generosity. Amen.*

Who Are You?

So what's all the fuss about self-image? I hope by now you know you have been blessed beyond measure. In the moments when you slump or fall into despair, remember who you are in Christ. You are never a nothing or a nobody. In 1 Peter 2:9, we discover the truth and the good news:

- you are a chosen generation
- you are a royal priesthood
- you are a holy nation
- you are God's special people

All of this was accomplished by Christ on your behalf. Although some people base their worth on accomplishments, as a Christian your identity is based on who you are in Christ. You have been chosen by God to be His very own. As a child of God—as one who has been purchased with the precious blood of Christ—you have worth that can never be measured. Thank God now!

Lord, forgive me for listening to my self-talk
more than I pay attention to Your bold
statements about my worth. I have value
because I am Your child. Thank You! Amen.

Wholehearted Work

Work, whether in or out of the home, is important to God. Why? Because your attitude toward work is a reflection of your attitude toward Him. God asks you to do your work heartily unto Him. You are also to serve your employers wholeheartedly and treat them fairly and with respect. Your obedience or disobedience to God's directives in the area of the workplace is easily seen—and noted!—by others.

Are people getting an accurate picture of the reality of Jesus Christ through your life? If you are truly pursuing a life of godliness, others will see the gospel in you. You are a witness to Christ (Acts 1:8). So...what's the gospel according to your life?

> *Master, even when my task is a simple one, You call me to a high standard. May I always remember that I am serving You and being a witness for You. Amen.*

How to Please God

The Word of God produces regeneration, but it is also an active force in our sanctification and in our purification. But you must do more than acknowledge the Bible as truth. What else is required?

- *Receive the Word.* Be quick to hear and to listen when the Bible is being taught.
- *Do and live the Word.* Put what you learn and know into practice daily.
- *Bridle your tongue.* Prayerfully plan to speak less and listen more.
- *Visit people in distress.* Actively care about and for people who are in need.
- *Live a godly lifestyle.* Strive to follow God's principles and live out His love and grace.

Oh, the beauty of a woman who puts her faith into action and controls her tongue, changes her behavior on the outside to honor God, and carries out God's guidelines on the inside!

> *Lord, I want to live my faith. Help me speak to and treat others in ways that reflect my living, active faith and commitment to You. May I be a faithful doer of Your Word. Amen.*

Be Approachable

Being approachable is a subtle quality. You may think, *Of course anyone could talk to me or ask something of me!* But you may also be conveying just the opposite attitude. Think again about Jesus' approachability. Are you sure you are approachable? To your husband and children? To the people at church, at work, or next door? Is your heart tuned in to those who are outcasts, hopeless, concerned, and needy, seemingly unimportant outsiders, even the insincere?

Jesus meant it when He said, "Come to Me, all you who labor and are heavy laden, and I will give you rest" (Matthew 11:28). Ask God for His love. Pray for an approachable spirit that will reflect the heart of Jesus, the One who never refuses the cries of anyone in need and sincerely seeking help…including you!

Lord Jesus, thank You that You have always been approachable in my times of need. May I reflect Your heart and be ready to receive others who need Your help through me. Amen.

Reflect the Big Heart of Jesus

In the Bible we witness Jesus' willingness to submit Himself to the Father and to becoming human—with all its limitations. He could be available to mankind as the perfect sacrifice even to the point of death. And His availability continues as "He is also able to save to the uttermost those who come to God through Him, since He always lives to make intercession for them" (Hebrews 7:25).

Jesus wants us to be available too. He doesn't want us to hoard our salvation and its resultant blessings. Instead, our Lord wants us to start up a conversation with others like the woman at the well (John 4:1-29). He gives us the grace to meet the needs of those who are suffering, like the woman with the 12-year illness (Matthew 9:20-22).

Make it a daily goal to be ready and available to reflect the big heart of Jesus.

> *O Father, may I remember Your complete*
> *availability to me when my heart cried*
> *out to You. Give me a heart that responds*
> *to the needs of others. Amen.*

Reach Out Today

Compassion and concern marked the Master's attitude toward those who were poor, unfortunate, and downcast. And Christ also showed concern for those who ministered alongside Him. We, too, should have this balanced compassion. For instance, sometimes we are quicker to experience and express compassion for the unfortunate and the helpless than we are for those who are spiritually mature and forging ahead in the Lord's work. Why is it we expect so much of those who are the church superheroes, those who are expected to keep on keeping on in ministry?

Who can you reach out to today in compassion? Pray to be on the lookout for those in need and to keep in mind the needs of those in the ministry. Such a prayer reminds us to put on a heart of compassion—to follow in Jesus' footsteps and have compassion for others.

Dear Jesus,
Fill my heart with compassion and care
For those who need help or live in despair.
Break my heart 'til it's able to see
Those who could use some kindness from me.
Amen.

Confidence in Christ

Confidence is a quality everyone desires and anyone can possess. You can take classes or receive special training to enable you to be more assertive, bold, and self-assured. But the confidence that comes from Christ and points to Him as its source is based on trust—trust in Him.

Are you placing your full trust in Jesus? Is your confidence at full strength, or have you lost sight of your identity with Christ? Are you confidently serving your family, raising your children, ministering your spiritual gifts, and being a bold witness with the authority of Christ? There is absolutely no reason for self-doubt or timidity. Redirect your focus to Jesus. You can have confidence in His absolute and unlimited authority. He is all you need for a bold confident life. Why? Because, as He explained to the disciples after His resurrection, "All authority has been given to Me in heaven and on earth" (Matthew 28:18). Go…with confidence!

*Thank You that I can live and serve with
confidence, knowing You are with me. Great are
You, Lord, and greatly to be praised! Amen.*

Your Courage Infusion

Jesus announced that "in the world you will have tribulation; but be of good cheer, I have overcome the world" (John 16:33). And He went on to urge His followers—including you—not to worry, because He will be with you. This fact, truth, and promise, all rolled into one, should bolster your courage.

Whether a tragedy strikes or your heart sinks in discouragement, you are never alone. Jesus is always with you and will never abandon you. As He told His disciples before He left them, "Lo, I am with you always, even to the end of the age" (Matthew 28:20).

Your precious, omnipresent Savior will go with you all the way through each trial...and all the way through life. He has overcome the world. Let His confidence infuse you with the courage to face life boldly as you live in and for Jesus Christ.

> *Lord Jesus, help me to recall Your powerful*
> *presence when I need to be courageous and*
> *live boldly as a Christian, to speak up when*
> *it's the right thing to do, and to stand up in*
> *the midst of difficult situations. Amen.*

Devoted and Disciplined

As you pause to consider your heart today, ask: Do I want to make a difference? Do I desire to positively influence those in my family, my circle of friends, my church, my workplace, and my community? If so, then following Jesus' example and living a more disciplined life is the way. To reflect Jesus and live out His purposes, embrace discipline as an essential element. Don't be like Eve, who failed to follow God because of a lack of self-control. Follow Abigail's excellent example of discipline and courage in word and deed. David said of Abigail: "Blessed is the Lord God of Israel, who sent you this day to meet me! And blessed is your advice and blessed are you, because you have kept me this day from coming to bloodshed and from avenging myself with my own hand" (1 Samuel 25:32-33). Make it your goal to become a model of discipline.

Lord Jesus, may I seek to live a pure life, to be
devoted to walking by Your Spirit in self-control.
May discipline become a reigning quality
in my life so You are glorified. Amen.

Nurturing Faithfulness

We have marveled at many instances of Jesus' faithfulness. And the good news is you can nurture and develop this same sterling quality. Call upon God in prayer. Count on Jesus' strength too. In Him you can do all things, including being faithful (Philippians 4:13). Ask God for His enabling grace to work at eliminating laziness and fulfilling one of His purposes for you—that you would be "faithful in all things" (1 Timothy 3:11).

God has already made available to you all that you require to be faithful. He has given you the Helper, the Holy Spirit. He has given you His Word, the Bible, to serve as a guide. And, praise upon praise, He has given you Jesus as a living model of faithfulness. Embrace our Savior's words: "He who is faithful in what is least is faithful also in much" (Luke 16:10). Start small, for faithfulness in a little thing is a great thing.

Lord Jesus, I want my love and service to be steadfast. I want to stand before You when my days on earth are done and hear You say, "Well done, good and faithful servant." Amen.

Seeking God's Plan

It's profoundly liberating to know your purpose in life. To drift aimlessly through your precious days is tiresome, frustrating, and unrewarding. It would be a great tragedy to wake up one day and realize all you could have accomplished if you had focused on some worthy goals along the way. You may already know your purpose. If so, focus your time and energies on it. But if you are a little behind or uncertain, spend time examining Jesus' life. Pay close attention to His focus and confidence as He lived God's purpose on a daily basis. Notice how He fixed His gaze on God's plan for Him. And be encouraged! As a woman who is seeking God's plan, you are already evidencing purpose. You are reflecting Jesus as you live out His instructions to "seek first the kingdom of God" (Matthew 6:33).

Blessed Jesus, help me discern how to use my time. My heart yearns to live for You and live out Your plan for me. Know my heart and lead the way. I want to follow! Amen.

A Forgiving Heart

Great confidence is yours when you know that you are forgiven in Christ! That forgiveness of sin produces life everlasting, which you began participating in from the moment of your salvation. When Christ is your Savior, God's Holy Spirit comes to reside in you. That means you can exhibit Christlike behavior (Galatians 5:22-23).

Here's how it works. Christ in you enables you to reflect Christlike character. For instance, it allows you to be long-suffering or to show patience. Long-suffering or patience refers to your ability to endure injuries inflicted by others and your willingness to accept annoying or painful situations. In Christ you are capable of not only withstanding great pain and suffering inflicted by others, but also of possessing the strength and power of Christ to forgive—with His love—those who cause the hurt.

Lord Jesus, thank You for forgiving my sin, and
helping me to forgive others. Let the beauty
of Your forgiveness wash over me. Give me the
love to forgive seventy times seven. Amen.

Having It All, Giving It All

Can you imagine having everything and yet being willing to give it all up? Well, that's the model that's presented to you and me in the life of Jesus. If you want to reflect the heart of Jesus and mirror His character, then generosity is a must. It's true that no one can out-give God, and if you are a child of God, you should desire to give and give generously to others. As Jesus told His disciples, "Freely you have received, freely give" (Matthew 10:8).

Think of all the blessings God has showered upon you. Salvation. The forgiveness of sin. The promise of eternal life. Like Jesus instructed the Twelve, you should freely give—not only your possessions and money, but your time, your help, your ministry, your mercy, and most of all, your love.

Lord Jesus, thank You that You gave the ultimate gift when You sacrificed Yourself to pay for my sins. May I, too, become a generous giver with no motives and no worries, only a desire to follow You and bless others. Amen.

The Power of Gentleness

No matter how society or those around you regard gentleness, it is an exquisite, powerful, and lofty Christlike attitude. To reflect this precious-in-the-sight-of-God quality, first desire it with all your heart. Then take every opportunity to bear mistreatment or misunderstanding with tranquility. Like Moses, fall on your face before God and wait for His action on your behalf. In prayer, seek His wisdom for your every move. Trust in the Lord to protect you and guide you, to empower you with His grace to respond to trials with Jesus' gentleness.

You will discover the might of gentleness as you live in the confidence, faithfulness, and compassion of Christ.

Lord Jesus, by Your grace may I accept what
happens in my life as part of Your purpose. May
I remember to trust You and count on Your love.
Thank You that each difficulty handled with
gentleness makes me more like You. Amen.

Doing Good in Christ

Jesus...went about doing good" (Acts 10:38). These five words inspire me every single day. I quote them to myself, fix them in my heart, and let them guide my deeds for one more day. Jesus accomplished so very much during His lifetime, and it all came from His goodness!

So pray daily for Christ's goodness to flow through you to others. Be on the lookout for opportunities to show His goodness in deeds of kindness. And once you spot an opportunity or think of something that would make someone else's days go better, don't stop! Put your observations and kind thoughts into action. Do everything Jesus brings to your mind to better the lives of others, to help lighten the load of the burdens they bear, to encourage faint hearts, and to lift their sorrows. Reflect the heart of Jesus by acting in goodness.

Good Teacher, help me to be less self-absorbed so I don't fail to notice those who are downcast or in need. Give me the grace to pour forth the riches of Your goodness as freely as You did. Amen.

Sharing God's Graciousness

Jesus was perfectly gracious. Because of His love, He was warm, courteous, and kind. He didn't merely turn on graciousness when needed and then just as easily turn it off. No, Jesus was gracious in nature. He was gracious all the time. That's how you can reflect the heart of Jesus. You reflect Him when your heart is filled with His love, and your lips overflow with gracious words. When you extend the gracious spirit of the Lord, people will feel welcome and cared for when they are in your presence. And best of all, your graciousness will draw people to Jesus as they are drawn to His reflection in you.

Gracious Lord, thank You for the wonderful, matchless grace You show toward me. Your love is completely undeserved and therefore full of grace. Please help me love You even more. And please enable me to extend Your loving, genuine grace to others. Amen.

Nurturing a Heart of Humility

How can you reflect a heart of humility? Think on Peter's words: "Humble yourselves under the mighty hand of God" (1 Peter 5:6). Each day, each act, and each word you speak is a fresh opportunity to cultivate Jesus' humility as a character quality. Humility does not rise from putting yourself down. No, it comes from knowing Christ and knowing your worth in Him. It takes place in the mind and heart and is referred to as "lowliness of mind" (Philippians 2:3). And it can and should be nurtured.

Reflect on Christ's great sacrifice on your behalf. When you follow this pattern, you will be humbled by the grace God has offered to you. Make willful choices that give humility expression. Talk less and listen more. Look for those who are suffering or alone and reach out.

And here's a biggie! Be a woman of prayer. Everything about prayer breeds humility.

Lord, I read about Your humility and am humbled
to the core. Please help me to choose to wrap
myself in the garment of humility, to focus on
others, and serve them in Your strength. Amen.

Abounding in Kindness

God, in His very nature, is kind. He responds to those who call on His name, including you. He is sympathetic to your situation and tender, warmhearted, and forbearing when it comes to your life and actions. As the Son of God, Jesus mirrored the Father and desires that you mirror Him too.

To accurately reflect Him, Jesus has a plan for you—to live a life "abounding with deeds of kindness and charity" (Acts 9:36 NASB). He desires in you a heart filled with a sincere kindness that goes beyond politeness. A simple act of thoughtfulness on your part can become an extraordinary blessing for the one receiving it...and for you. Kindness is a characteristic of one of God's people, and when you are kind, you display the character of Christ to a watching world, allowing others to catch a glimpse of Jesus.

> *Dear Jesus, I desire to live a life of kindness, and to imitate Your compassion, benevolence, and forgiving attitude. Create in me a sympathy for those who are less fortunate, who are in pain or need. And may I give You glory, Lord. Amen.*

Reaching Out in Love

Have you ever thought about why Jesus commands you to love? Love takes effort. It must be nudged a bit, especially if you are hesitating when it comes to reaching out in love, maybe because you were hurt at some time as you tried loving another person.

If for some reason or other you find yourself hesitant to obey God's command to love, you need to recall how deeply you are loved by Jesus in spite of your sins and faults. His unconditional love should move you to love others. It shows you the way to love. Realizing how much God loves you will begin to remove your difficulties in loving others. Then, as you practice love toward others, the feelings of love will follow naturally. You will find yourself reflecting the heart of Jesus as you reach out in love—just like He did.

> *Precious Jesus, I thank You for the gift of love You extended to me in salvation—a gift I could not earn or repay. And I thank You, Father, that I can love You because You first loved me. Amen.*

Blessing Awaits

For Jesus, prayer was like breathing. It was as if He couldn't live without it. His one desire was to fulfill the Father's will. In His last recorded prayer to the Father before He was nailed to the cross, He said, "I have glorified You on the earth. I have finished the work which You have given Me to do" (John 17:4). How was He able to do this? Prayer! Jesus prayed to accomplish the goal of fulfilling God's will.

All the blessings of prayer await you. The blessings of communing with God. The blessings of dealing with sin and growing more into the image of Jesus. The blessings of taking decisions and needs to God. And the blessings of loving others and asking God to work in their lives. Best of all, building the habit of daily prayer builds Christlike character into your life...which leads to the blessing of reflecting the great heart of Jesus!

> *Jesus, I acknowledge the need, importance,*
> *and blessings of being a woman of prayer. Help*
> *me to "do it," to become a woman after Your*
> *heart who prays faithfully as You did. Amen.*

Live for Him

You and I, as women of God, have a lot of responsibilities to our families, churches, neighbors, friends, and our Lord. How do we manage all of these? Once again, we can look to Jesus as our model, our hope, and our strength. He fulfilled all His responsibilities to the very end, to the very last responsibility—going to the cross to pay the penalty for sin. This was indeed the ultimate act of responsibility for all time.

Where is fulfilling your responsibilities to the Father taking you? God is not asking you to die for Him. He is asking you to live for Him, to be a "living sacrifice" (Romans 12:1). Jesus possessed a heart of obedience that made Him responsible. If you desire to reflect the heart of Jesus, make it a priority to nurture a heart that is responsible to obey God and follow the example of His Son, the Lord Jesus.

> *Dear Lord Jesus, my heart's desire is to become more like You. As I learn about responsibility, I want my attitudes and actions to demonstrate that I am a living sacrifice, wholly acceptable to You. Amen.*

Sensing Needs and Submitting

Many people came to Jesus for assistance, and He was available and helpful to them. And in His love and grace, He demonstrated great sensitivity when He went looking for those who needed His healing touch, His words of encouragement and instruction, or the assurance of His presence in their lives as they faced the future. You can do what Jesus did. Open your eyes and heart—and reach out willingly!

Jesus will always show you how to live the best way, His way—the path of submission. When you cease looking for ways to satisfy selfish interests, you will be free to wholeheartedly yield to Jesus and His ways. You will be able to sense and serve the needs of others. As you start submitting to Jesus, you will find it much easier to submit to others. It is then that you will truly reflect the submissive heart of Jesus.

Dear Jesus, You show me how to love, serve, and submit. It comes from the heart—Your heart. May my love shine brightly so others see You in my good deeds, obedience, and submission. Amen.

A Heart Attitude of Service

Following in the steps of Jesus involves developing the heart attitude of serving. And this noble quality begins at home with your family. If you are married, God has given you the assignment of being your husband's "helper" (Genesis 2:18). That means your husband becomes God's priority person to receive your ministry of service. And if you have children, they are number two on your list of people to serve. Beyond this calling you are to serve all, to "serve one another" (Galatians 5:13).

When you are serving others, your heartfelt, Spirit-filled service is a dazzling reflection of the heart of your Savior, the greatest servant who ever lived, the One who set the standard when He served others, whether or not they deserved it or thanked Him. Jesus always served with sacrificial love and calls us to do the same.

O Lord, when my heart tires of serving, remind me of Yourself and Your holy hands washing the disciples' feet! May I become Your twin in selflessly tending to the needs of others. Amen, and thank You!

Every Day Is Thanksgiving

Traditionally a Thanksgiving Day celebration is associated with giving thanks and expressing gratitude to God for the harvest of His bounty and provision. Praise and thanksgiving should not be reserved for one day. Exalting God and giving thanks should be part of every day. Thank Him before you rise. Thank Him for each meal. Thank Him for family, friends, a good church, and His provision.

Thanks should flow from your lips for God and His gift of Jesus *and* for people God places in your path. Also thank these people directly—parents, friends, church leaders, and immediate family. God has used these people to mold and shape you into the woman you are today—a woman who reflects the heart of Jesus.

> *Lord, I come to You with a heart of gratitude. In the words of King David, I marvel, "Who am I, O Lord God" that You have blessed me so abundantly?" (2 Samuel 7:18). Every day I will offer You praise and thanksgiving. Amen!*

God's To-Do List

Jesus had a to-do list from the Father, and He woke up every day to take care of that list. His checked-off chores looked like this:

- keep the law
- serve and minister to the people
- go to the people and preach the gospel
- go to Jerusalem…and go to the cross
- fulfill all of the Father's will

As a woman, you also have a to-do list from God, which includes taking care of yourself and your family, home, ministry, and work. As you pray over your list, remember Jesus. Let His faithfulness show you the way through your days.

> *Lord, a part of me faints at the thought of being*
> *virtuous and pursuing excellence in all things. But*
> *You have shown me the way. You have walked*
> *it before me. Help me to walk in it. Amen!*

The Wise Woman

Unlike Jesus, you will not always make perfect choices and decisions. But when you choose to submit to the Father's will and follow His lead, you will reflect the heart of Jesus. You will find yourself viewing life from His perspective. You will begin choosing better courses of action. You will be blessed by the results of the wisdom you are applying, and so will the others in your life. You will become the woman you want to be—a woman of wisdom. You will also become "the wise woman [who] builds her house...[who] opens her mouth with wisdom" (Proverbs 14:1; 31:26).

> *My Lord, You are "the wisdom of God"*
> *(1 Corinthians 1:24). You grew in wisdom,*
> *walked in wisdom, spoke wisdom, and*
> *lived wisely. You have set a pattern for me*
> *to follow. May the choices I make and the*
> *words I speak reflect Your wisdom. Amen.*

God's Grace

Do you know that the sustaining power of God is packaged in His grace? Life can deliver some tough blows, but God's marvelous grace enables us to go from strength to strength through all the trials. Second Corinthians 12:9 promises that God's grace is sufficient—that it is made perfect in our weakness. I know that encourages my heart. Take that trial you're experiencing and bring it to the Lord. Lay it at His feet. Look to Him. Count on His grace and power in every situation. It's there. It's given to you. And it brings the peace you so long for.

Bless you in your journey to become a woman after God's own heart.

Father, my heart overflows with the love and blessings You've given me. Even in the midst of my trials and sorrow, I can be joyful in my heart because I know You are in charge. Amen.

The Things of God

Redeeming your time is so important. What do I mean? Time is redeemed when you make the most of your life by fulfilling God's purposes. As you line up your life and seize every opportunity for useful service, your life takes on an efficient quality. That may be difficult to imagine since you're so busy, but as you focus on doing the business of God, time expands. I don't know who wrote this poem, but it's so true:

> I have only just a minute.
> Only sixty seconds in it.
> Just a tiny little minute.
> But eternity is in it.

As your heart becomes more dedicated to God, you'll reclaim, recover, retrieve, rescue, and regain the minutes, hours, and days of your life for His glory.

> *Jesus, what a precious gift time is! Please keep me aware of my stewardship of this great award. Help me make good use of every hour, realizing that once spent, it can never be returned to me. Amen.*

Guard Your Time

What stole your day from you today? Was it putting off something you knew you should do? Something important for living out God's plan for your life? It's been said, "If you don't plan your day, someone else will plan it for you." Who's the best person to create your schedule? You, of course! Who has prayed through your priorities and desires to do God's will? It's you again, dear friend. Don't let someone who is clueless about your goals and your God-given desires and priorities plan your day. God has given you today to serve Him. Plan your day. Schedule your day. Protect your day.

> *Lord, surely You have set the hours of my day*
> *before me. Help me guard them diligently,*
> *making the most of each moment. Give me*
> *wisdom as I plan the many details of my busy*
> *life. Most of all, keep me mindful of You in*
> *the midst of everything I have to do. Amen.*

A "Today" Resolution

You don't have to wait until New Year's Day to make a resolution about your schedule. Why not make one today? First, pray over your priorities: "Lord, what is Your will for me at this time of my life?" Now plan through your priorities and prepare a schedule: "Lord, when should I do the things that live out these priorities today?" Ask the Lord to give you direction for your day: "Lord, I only have a limited time left in my day. What do I need to focus on?" Prepare for tomorrow: "Lord, how can I better live out Your plan for my life?" Let the Lord know you appreciate Him: "Lord, thank You for this day…and the opportunity to talk with You directly." Then go forth with confidence and joy.

*Lord, my life is Yours. I want to please You
in everything I do. I need Your guidance and
strength and stamina. I love You. Amen.*

118

A Present for You

I want to give you two presents right now: the gift of encouragement…and applause for a job well done in caring for your home. As one person put it, "The greatest priority in a home should be love. If a wife loves her husband and her children, she is well on the way to making the marriage and the home a success." Proverbs 9:1 says, "Wisdom has built her house, she has hewn out her seven pillars." It took me a while to discover there's no greater task, responsibility, and privilege in this world than to make a house a home. I know that takes work, which is not always appreciated. I truly honor what it takes to be a woman, a wife, and a mother today. Thank you for all you do to take care of yourself and your family. I pray that God will continue to bless you richly.

Lord, I thank You for the house I call home. Give me insight and wisdom in making my home reflect Your presence. You are welcome here! Amen.

A Special Time

Why not plan a special night for your family? If you're not married, get friends together. Give everyone plenty of notice, especially if teens are involved. When the time comes around, prepare a festive meal, go out to dinner, or order pizza!

Later, gather around and have everyone share what they've done in the past three months that was fun and meaningful. Encourage each person to share a goal or dream…and be supportive. Dreams aren't always based on current reality. Talk about the childhood antics of the kids, how you and your husband grew up, what your parents did, and where your grandparents lived. Share your faith experiences…and let others share theirs. End your time together by drawing people's names out of a hat and committing to doing two nice things for that person during the week.

Lord, You've given me a wonderful family
and awesome friends. I delight in being with
these people You've given me to cherish…and
I especially delight in You. Amen.

No More Gossip

"No more gossip." What an admirable goal! One of the most common questions I get from women centers around gossiping: "How can I avoid sharing it and listening to it?" Philippians 4:8 says, "Whatever things are true…noble…just…pure…meditate on these things." In other words, think godly thoughts about others. And if any of your thoughts about others don't measure up to God's guidelines, they're out! Confess them, deal with them, and be done with them. A powerful truth is that if we love the Lord, love His Word, love His people, and love one another, we won't want to gossip. It's that simple…and that important.

Lord, You hate gossip! You abhor words that diminish another person. Help me look at others through Your eyes and think only the best about them, especially when awkward situations arise. I don't want others to gossip about me, so I choose not to gossip about them. Amen.

Love Is a Decision

Loving your husband is a daily choice. Love may start out as a good feeling, but to love someone long-term is an act of the will. It means loving someone even when he may not be lovable at that particular moment. Hopefully your husband is your best friend. Enjoy being with him. Spoil him. Think about him. Pray for him. Encourage him.

But what if you don't feel this way? The question remains, "Will you love your husband?" Do everything you can—starting right now—to restore your love. Pray for him. Do little acts of kindness for him. Express your love in every way you can. Thoughtful deeds and kind thoughts will reenergize your love and revitalize your marriage. Love is blossoming in you, my friend.

Lord, loving another person can sometimes be trying. But by Your grace I can love my spouse completely. I choose to honor and serve this man I call husband. Help me be the wife he needs. Work in his life so he will be all You envisioned. Amen.

Your Attitudes and Actions

Family is the best place to teach young men and women about God's kind of love. Today, let's focus on your daughters. Titus 2:3-5 says we're to teach our daughters, our granddaughters, and our younger sisters in Christ the good things in the Christian life, including how to love a husband. What are you modeling in your marriage? Don't be afraid to be affectionate in front of your kids. Let them see and hear that you love your husband. Compliment your spouse and let your kids know you trust and respect him. Don't disparage or nag him. Deal with disagreements privately. Show your children that making sacrifices for another person isn't drudgery. Share scriptures that encourage you and help you live out God's calling as a woman, a wife, a mother.

Lord, marriage is a model of Your love for Your church. May my marriage be representative of that same sacrificial love You have for us. May my family reflect Your values and priorities. And may others see in us the beauty of Christian love. Amen.

The Hardest Work

Raising kids can be an uphill battle. I know that from experience! Although we love them dearly, they aren't always the little angels we wish they'd be. When we don't feel very loving, does that mean we're being bad mothers? No! We're human…and God knows that. A godly mother loves God with all her heart, soul, mind, and strength. And she passionately and consistently teaches her children to do the same. No one has more potential for godly influence on your children than you and your husband. Pray every day for these little ones and pour God's Word into their lives. Ask God to give you wisdom as you show your kids you love them. Amid the joy of raising children will be some of the hardest life work you'll ever do. And it's one of God's highest callings. Hang in there!

*Father, I need Your strength, grace, and mercy as
I deal with my kids today. I want to shower them
with unconditional love and support. And I want
to open their minds and hearts to You. Amen.*

The Beginning of Wisdom

Doesn't being a "wise woman" sound a bit like being an "ancient woman"? And we're definitely not there yet! Well, wisdom doesn't necessarily have a thing to do with age. I pray every day for wisdom in my life. I want a life characterized by peace and joy, by order and meaning. Does this sound too good to be true? There's no getting around the fact that a godly life is lived one minute at a time, one thought at a time, one decision at a time. Proverbs 9:10 says, "The fear of the LORD is the beginning of wisdom, and the knowledge of the Holy One is understanding."

My friend, if you have a heart for God, read His Word. God is knowledge and God is wisdom. Live according to His high calling.

Father, You are the source of all wisdom.
Whenever I am faced with a choice, a
decision, a responsibility, may I look to You
and Your Word for guidance. Amen.

Thou Shalt Be Organized

Are you continually looking for your car keys? Have you misplaced your glasses, the remote control, or important paperwork again? How much of your day is spent searching for lost items? Careful planning eliminates a lot of stress. So plan ahead as much as possible. Set aside special places for your things. Hang your keys on a special hook (but not by the door!).

Create a decorative box for the remote. Get a monthly bill-paying system up and running. I work off a list I carry with me. And no, not everything gets done, but more gets done than if I didn't have a list!

Organization is more than just physical. Give careful thought to your schedule so you have time for spontaneity. Allow time for God to take you in a new direction or show you someone in need.

There are few feelings better than feeling organized. Take the plunge!

Lord, I'm constantly wasting time looking for things.
By being organized I'll have more time for the work
You have for me. I'll start on it today! Amen.

How's Your Attitude?

As you rush to and fro running errands, picking up the kids, getting to work, buying groceries…do you keep a positive attitude? Or do frustration and irritation take over? When I'm frazzled, I tend to let go. Losing my temper comes very easily to me, along with the desire— and sometimes the action!—to tell someone exactly how I feel and what I think. But I want to practice what I preach. And believe me, it sometimes takes all of God's strength in my life to help me do…nothing! To not react. I continually ask God to fill me with His love and patience, two key elements the Bible calls fruit of the Spirit (Galatians 5:22-23). We're called on to exhibit the same loving patience Jesus had. And how busy we are doesn't fit into the equation.

Lord, when things don't go as planned or something interferes with my day, I get so frustrated. Help me be more flexible. And give me the wisdom and grace to respond in love to the people involved. Amen.

Joy and Rejoicing

Is this it? Is this all there is to life? When does the fun start?" Do you feel this way? My friend, God's Word can cheer you like nothing else. The prophet Jeremiah reported, "Your words were found…and Your word was to me the joy and rejoicing of my heart" (Jeremiah 15:16). Rush to the Word of the Lord. God's peace and perspective are available to you now even when grief and gloom are part of your day. The Bible will teach you, correct you, instruct you, guide you, and, yes, cheer you up and give you hope. Make the heart of your life for God a passion for His Word. Spend your time learning about Jesus. This is what you need for your life journey!

Lord, I'm bogged down. My days seem dreary and mundane. I'm going to read Your Word today. Open my mind and heart to Your wisdom, Your love, and Your purpose for my life. Thank You. Amen.

A Unique Boundary

We all need to take time for ourselves, time to revitalize, reenergize, recoup, and refresh. But may I suggest a unique boundary? A dear friend of mine—a brave one, I might add—shared her discipline in the Word. Donna doesn't allow herself to spend more time in any personal activity each day than she spends in the Word of God. She passed this principle on to me, and I've made it part of my life too. A word of warning! If you get serious about establishing this practice, your life, your priorities, your schedule, and your interests are going to change.

Is that the ground I hear rumbling?

Lord, in my heart I want to make You my first priority, but I don't always follow through when it comes to my thoughts and actions. Help me to guard my time with You more jealously. Amen.

Pray, My Friend

I'd pray more often, but I run out of stuff to say." I can certainly relate. To grow in the Lord, the reading and studying of God's Word is essential. And so is prayer. In fact, prayer is one of the privileges we have as Christians.

The Bible calls us to a life of faithful prayer, which isn't always easy. One of the best incentives to pray is that it strengthens us and short-circuits our tendency to sin. Prayer also gives us the strength and wisdom to follow through on the teachings in the Bible.

If prayer is difficult for you, set aside a small amount of time for prayer every day. Gradually increase that time as you settle into this routine. And you can talk to God about anything. No question, no problem, no concern is too big or too small for Him to handle!

Lord, calm my spirit as I come to You with praise and share my concerns. Give me the courage to talk to You and the patience to listen for Your response. Amen.

Be Careful, Little Mind

Are you dreaming of an ice cream sundae? Or maybe yearning for designer jeans? Perhaps you're tempted by forbidden fruit? Ah, dear friend, you have control over what you think—and you must engage this power! What exactly does this mean? Answer: Disciplining those thoughts of yours. There's a nursery song my kids used to sing: "Be careful, little mind, what you think." That says it all! You've got to be careful and guard your mind against thoughts that might lead you down sin's path. "Sow a thought, reap an action" is sage advice. Our actions, habits, character, and future are definitely affected by our thoughts. Colossians 3:1-2 says to "seek those things which are above" and to "set your mind on things above, not on things on the earth." Aim your thoughts higher and higher. And "be careful, little mind, what you think."

My thoughts go astray often, Lord. Sometimes
I'm not even sure where these questionable
thoughts come from! Help me meditate on
Your love and the tremendous joy following
Your precepts gives me. Amen.

Spiritual Nip and Tuck

I've come to the point in my spiritual growth that I believe strongly that if my physical life is important to God, it should also be important to me. But how far should I take this? What are good guidelines? Makeover TV shows and the widespread use of cosmetic surgery exploit the attitude that "this is my body, and I can do with it as I please." But this couldn't be more wrong! God owns our bodies. They're not ours. The body of a believer is to be used for God's glory. Our behavior and the way we talk should reflect positively on Him (1 Corinthians 6:20).

Face-lifts and such aren't specifically banned, but make sure vanity and pride aren't the roots of your desire. Concentrate on becoming physically fit and active. Find something you can do with your husband, your kids, or your friends. And while you're out there exercising, keep your eyes and ears open for opportunities to share your faith in Jesus!

Jesus, make me over in Your image. I want to become more like You every day. In everything I do, I want to honor You. Amen.

Heaven on Earth

Would you describe what goes on in your home as "heaven on earth"? That's quite an expression, isn't it? Heaven on earth! Do you know that your home life is meant to be exactly that? The Bible uses home life and marriage as illustrations of God's relationship with His church, with the people who choose to follow Him. And when you live out your God-ordained roles and fulfill your God-given assignments, others take notice and see proof of our special relationship with the Lord.

You have the privilege of presenting a picture of what heaven will be like to those around you. When you pursue with passion and purpose God's design for a woman, a homemaker, a wife, or a mother, you establish a home that reflects the order and beauty of life in heaven. An amazing opportunity, isn't it?

*I'm only human, Lord. How can I have a home
and marriage that reflects Your perfect love,
Your perfect peace? I want to grow in these
areas. I want to point people to You. Amen.*

All Things Are New

Before I accepted Christ, I did my own thing. I did what I wanted and chased after my goals. And my marriage and family suffered. By God's grace I accepted Christ in my late twenties—and it saved my marriage. Second Corinthians 5:17 says, "If anyone is in Christ, [she] is a new creation; old things have passed away; behold, all things have become new." Suddenly, for the first time in my life, I had something in my life to empower me. I felt worthwhile and truly alive. I earnestly started seeking God's will for my life. Through His Word I'm discovering more and more about what it means to be a woman after God's own heart. As I share that knowledge with you and we grow in the Lord together, I hope you're encouraged to study the Bible on your own too.

Heavenly Father, thank You for my salvation and my new life in Christ. Every day I want to learn more about You so I can live according to Your plan and share Your great love with others. Amen.

"I Do!"

Is your marriage growing a bit stale? Are you stuck in a marriage rut? This might be a good time to think back and recall why you said "I do" in the first place. Remember those crazy things you did when you were dating? The laughter? The fun? The way to recapture those happier days is by making sure each day involves the same lighthearted joy. Proverbs 5:18 says a husband and wife are to continually rejoice in one another.

Here are a few tips to help in that direction. They're right out of Scripture, so we know they'll work! Sprinkled through the book of Proverbs are these caveats: Don't be contentious, don't nag, and don't embarrass your husband by your speech, your appearance, or your behavior. Are you wondering what your husband's responsibilities are? That's between him and God. Right now God wants you to concentrate on you!

> *Dear Jesus, give me guidance in ways*
> *I can keep my marriage healthy…and*
> *growing…and loving…and fun. I also*
> *want it to be centered on You. Amen.*

Humble Yourself

English preacher Charles Haddon Spurgeon said, "Humility is the proper estimate of oneself." Humility begins when we know ourselves. Yes, we're made in the image of God, but Romans 3:23 reminds us, "For all have sinned and fall short of the glory of God." Romans 12:2 tells us, "Do not be conformed to this world, but be transformed by the renewing of your mind, that you may prove what is that good and acceptable and perfect will of God." This renewing is done through faithful praying, when we bow before God, confessing our sins, thanking and praising Him for all He's done for us. And then we can strive to imitate Christ's humbleness. And humility also includes respecting others by serving them and considering them better than ourselves. It's a tall order, but we can do all things through Christ!

Father, I don't like to think of myself as selfish or better than others, but sometimes what I do communicates that. Help me focus on You so I can present You to others without me getting in the way. Amen.

That One Thing

You may have heard the expression, "But one thing I do…" What is that "one thing" in your life? In Philippians 3:13-14, the apostle Paul said his "one thing" was to forget what is behind and reach forward to what's ahead, pressing on toward the goal to win the prize of the upward call of God in Christ Jesus. I encourage you to be like a runner—never looking back at the ground already covered, but instead moving forward deliberately. According to Paul's example, we should concentrate our energies on moving forward into the future.

Where are you putting your focus? Have your goal in view—and keep your eyes, your heart, and your life fixed on the end of the race. We conquer by continuing…so press on!

> *Father, thank You for forgiving me and taking care of my past…and my future! Help me look ahead to see how I can serve You and run the course You've set before me. Amen.*

God's Peace and Joy

Do you struggle with depression? With negative thoughts? God promises you joy. No matter what your circumstances, you can have joy in Him. Philippians 4:4 says, "Rejoice in the Lord always. Again I will say, rejoice!" Rejoicing is not an option. And the truth is that the kind of rejoicing the Bible talks about often comes from a life of pain and hardship. But God's peace and joy will prevail. Philippians 4:6-7 says, "Be anxious for nothing, but in everything by prayer and supplication, with thanksgiving, let your requests be made known to God; and the peace of God, which surpasses all understanding, will guard your hearts and minds through Christ Jesus." God's peace stands guard against all those things that attack your mind and heart. Through prayer you'll also experience the joy God gives—His joy—in abundance (John 17:13).

Father, You are an awesome God! You not only give me the strength and fortitude I need to make it through my trials, but You also shower me with Your joy and peace along the way. Thank You! Amen.

The Flawless Word of God

How gullible are you? I'm not asking in a derogatory or put-down way. I tend to believe what I hear, read, and watch. If you're like me, you realize there's definitely a need to discern truth. And that ability comes from learning, growing, and understanding the Bible. You may want to get involved in a Bible study or take some classes to further your knowledge. Memorizing Scripture is crucial to being able to separate fact from fiction. The American Banking Association once sponsored a training program to help tellers detect counterfeit bills. Not once during the training were the tellers exposed to actual counterfeits. For two weeks they handled nothing but the real thing. They became so familiar with the "true" that they couldn't be fooled by the false. And that's exactly what I'm encouraging you to do!

Jesus, memorizing takes time and energy,
which are in short supply in my life. Please
give me an energy boost and open my mind to
Your Word. I want to do everything I can to
know truth and learn about You! Amen.

Second Fiddle

An interviewer asked famed conductor Leonard Bernstein, "What's the most difficult instrument to play?" Good-naturedly he replied, "Second fiddle!" Then he added, "And if no one plays second, there's no harmony." We need to be more than willing to be God's servants. We need to revel in the opportunities He gives us to serve.

Do you have someone you work with, serve with shoulder to shoulder? A woman you help as she serves the Lord? The apostle Paul said of Timothy in Philippians 2:19-20, "I trust in the Lord Jesus to send Timothy to you shortly...I have no one like-minded, who will sincerely care for your state." I pray that you'll spend time with a mentor in ministry and in prayer and Bible study. I encourage you to mature in your usefulness. Be content to play "second fiddle."

Jesus, You were so humble and willing to serve. I want to follow Your example. Keep me from being caught up in wanting to be in charge of everything. Help me look for places to serve and uplift others. Amen.

God's Dress Code

If you're working out and 'lookin' good,' why not show it off?" That's a great question! And I've got a copy of God's "dress code" sitting right here in front of me. It's found in 1 Timothy 2:9, and it couldn't be clearer: "I also want women to dress modestly, with decency and propriety, not with braided hair or gold or pearls or expensive clothes, but with good deeds, appropriate for women who profess to worship God" (NIV). *Modesty. Propriety.* These two words are rare these days…both in speech and in media. If you profess godliness, your actions and your appearance should reflect your values. Good works are a great adornment for women who love God.

> *Jesus, I don't want to be old-fashioned, but I do want to please You. Give me discernment in how to dress so I represent You well. Thank You for Your free gift of salvation. Help me see opportunities to do good so people will be encouraged to seek You. Amen.*

The Fickleness of Praise

Faithfulness is a high calling. And you and I will have our reward if we serve well. So hang in there while doing good deeds and serving others. We're in this Christian life for the long haul. Yes, it's nice to be recognized for what we do, but that's not always going to happen. Our focus is on serving as representatives of Christ, sharing His love and concern and provision, not personal recognition.

As women we're in unique positions to reflect the softer, gentler side of faith in the Lord. We can show how kind and generous hearts, tempered by wisdom and strength, come from God. As we serve, we reflect His unconditional love. What an awesome privilege!

When all is said and done, one of our rewards may be praise, but the greater reward is being faithful to follow our Lord and Savior, Jesus Christ.

> *Lord, my ego likes it when people praise me for something I've done. Remind me always to give You credit. My gifts and the abilities to love and help others come directly from You. Amen.*

Love the Sinner

A loving heart attitude is at the core of caring for others. When a friend sins, it's okay to hate her sin—in fact, that's a biblical principle. But we're to continue to love the sinner unconditionally. We are not to rejoice in another person's suffering or downfall, being glad that she "got what was coming to her." Jesus said in Matthew 12:34, "Out of the abundance of the heart the mouth speaks." Here's a little checkup you won't find in your doctor's office, but it could go a long way in keeping you spiritually healthy. John 13:34 says, "Love one another." Ephesians 6:18 says to pray for one another. Philippians 2:3 encourages us to respect one another. First Thessalonians 5:11 says to comfort and "edify one another." How's your heart? Are you living these biblical mandates?

Father, it's so natural to be petty, to be glad when someone who seems high-and-mighty is brought low. But that's not Your way. That's not how You love. I want to love unconditionally and purely like You. Show me how. Amen.

Parents, In-Laws, and You

Today I want to go beyond the "God calls you to love" admonition and have a heart-to-heart with you about your parents and in-laws. Jim and I decided long ago that our parents were high priorities. We purposed to do everything we could for them. While they were younger, this didn't involve much. We visited regularly and kept in touch. As they got older, their challenges were greater, and we had many chances to serve. When Jim's mother's health failed, we willingly spent our time and resources to help her. When she died, we had no regrets because we'd been there for her. The same applied to my father, and again as we, along with my siblings, watched out for my mother. Caring for our parents takes time, yes, and it takes money and effort. But it's well worth it...and pleases God!

Father, it's such a privilege to serve You.
And I'm glad You've given me my parents and
in-laws to love. Help me be patient, kind,
and generous with my time and resources. Amen.

Pray for Your Children

Praying for your children is the most powerful way you can care for them. Most times your heart will naturally overflow in prayer for them. And even when they're causing trouble or your patience is wearing thin, a quick prayer will calm your nerves and soothe your children. You'll be amazed at the huge difference prayer will make in the lives of your little ones. Ask God to show you how to let them know that after Him and your husband, they're more important than all the other people in your life.

Be ready to show your love. Set aside time each day to pray for your kiddos. And don't forget to pray for them when they're around. That lets them know you and God love them. It also models prayer and helps them feel more secure.

Praying for your kids is some of the best time you'll ever invest. Prayer is a powerful privilege!

Jesus, protect these little lives You've placed in my care. Help me be patient, calm, loving, and supportive. Open their hearts to You. Amen.

A New Woman

I'm sure you've been in grocery stores, libraries, and even parks where the kids were really wild. They didn't listen to their parents and generally created havoc. I can relate to the parents of those unruly kids. Raising children didn't come easily for me, and in the early days of my marriage, our home was chaotic. Thankfully, Jesus came into our lives! When we became a Christian family, our girls were almost two and three years old. God—and His wonderful Word—came to our aid with practical guidelines for raising kids and creating a loving home. My life, my marriage, and my home were transformed as Jim and I, and eventually our girls, grew spiritually. I encourage you to use your Bible's index or get a concordance and search out the keys to a calm, loving home. Also talk with seasoned moms. You and your family will reap the rewards!

Father, I'm totally awed by what You've accomplished in my life. Your guidance and wisdom have made such a difference! I don't even want to imagine what life would be like without You. I praise Your holy name! Amen.

Love Your Home

Are you tired of doing dishes, sweeping and vacuuming floors, dusting, and picking up after other people? I can so relate. But it is worth it! Or at least it can be. You and I know that love is the world's most powerful motivator. So love your home—love being there and love managing it, watching over it, keeping it, and yes, cleaning up the mess. Love will enable you and empower you to tackle it, master it, and excel at it. Turn to the Lord to fire up your passion in your heart to manage your home His way...in a loving, serving, sacrificial capacity. No task will be too difficult and no job will be meaningless with Him as the foundation.

Heavenly Father, sometimes I get tired of the mundane aspects of being a woman, wife, and mom. But I love You, my family, and my home. Help me find meaning in the little things that keep my life on Your path. Amen.

When You're Overwhelmed

So many women I talk to feel overwhelmed. With responsibilities at school, church, home, and on the job, there's just too much to do. I've probably just described your life, haven't I? Believe me, doing all that and trying to fit in Bible studies and worship and other activities related to being a Christian is no easy task. But you know what? The Old Testament shows us the way through Abraham. The Bible says he responded immediately to the call of God (Genesis 12:1-4; Hebrews 11:8). He trusted the Lord, and he moved out in obedience. What an encouragement to us! Whether the task at hand seems doable or not, the miracle of God occurs after we act in faith. Decide to do what God is asking of you. That's when you'll truly know His provision!

*Heavenly Father, today I'm going to step out
in faith and willingly and joyfully do all I feel
You are calling me to do. I know You'll give me
the strength and time. Thank You. Amen.*

I Shall Not Want

When is your church's next retreat? How long until your Bible study group gets together for fellowship? Do you catch an occasional radio broadcast or do quick devotional readings once in a while? Too often we neglect nurturing our spiritual lives, hoping to get by on quick fixes. If your desire is to grow spiritually, you'll need to spend quality time in God's Word and more time in prayer.

I love Psalm 23, which starts, "The LORD is my shepherd; I shall not want." This so reminds me of my need for Him. Are you following the Shepherd? "He makes me to lie down in green pastures; He leads me beside the still waters. He restores my soul; He leads me in the paths of righteousness for His name's sake" (verses 2-3). Are you lying down in green pastures as the verse says? Are you feeding to your heart's content on His provision?

Father, You are my Shepherd. I want to follow
You all of my days on earth…and into eternity.
Restore my soul and refresh my spirit today. Amen.

Where He Leads

What would you do if God suddenly called you to a different ministry? Sometime when you have a few minutes for yourself, take a card and write these words: *anything, anywhere, anytime, at any cost.* Then date the note. Can you in all honesty sign it? God's role is to lead us. Our job is to follow.

How are you doing? Have you looked into God's wonderful face and into His eyes of love and whispered, "Truly, dear Lord, where You lead me, I will follow"? Do these words express the deep longing of your heart? Are you following Him today? If not, will you?

> *God, You are my reason for living, my salvation, my comfort, my provider, my love. I choose today to follow You every step of the way. When the way gets hard and I falter, encourage me and give me strength. Amen.*

Meek to Mighty

I used to be so confident. But now I feel like such a loser." Do you feel this way? My friend, God never asks for us to have confidence. He only asks that we have confidence in Him! And when God commands, He also supplies. This is true for every area of your life.

In Old Testament times, the Midianites periodically destroyed the crops of the children of Israel. A young man named Gideon secretly "threshed wheat in the winepress, in order to hide it from the Midianites" (Judges 6:11). He doesn't sound very brave, does he? And yet we learn that God enabled and strengthened the meek Gideon into a mighty warrior, a man of valor, a man of mighty faith (Hebrews 11:32-33).

God will transform you too. Yield to Him. Trust Him. Allow Him to do great things in and through and for you.

Father God, when I'm hesitant to show faith in You, give me courage and the right words to say that will lead people to You. Open doors for me to bravely serve You and share Your truths. Amen.

The Strength to Go On

Some hardships in life are devastating. The death of a husband, child, or parent, divorce, disappointment, betrayal…all are very difficult situations. How do you go on when tragedy strikes? How do you handle what life throws at you? The good news is that God will come to the rescue. His tender care goes into action with His promise to heal us. I love these four words in Psalm 23:3 that speak to my heart: "He restores my soul." Our wonderful Lord not only takes care of our physical needs, but He also takes care of our spiritual needs. Isn't that uplifting? You can have hope in whatever your situation because He is a mighty and compassionate and loving God who will restore your soul. Hallelujah!

Father God, there's so much pain and suffering in this world…and I feel it too. It's hard to understand why life has to be so hard, but I'm so thankful I know You. You give me the strength to endure and still praise You. Amen.

A Model for the Home

The woman of Proverbs 31 is a great model for home management. She does her husband good. She makes household items for her family and to sell. She shops wisely. She's very industrious. She buys land, plants crops, and invests. She keeps herself fit. This woman helps the needy. She's honorable, wise, and kind. She looks forward to the future. And her children and husband sing her praises. And no wonder!

Look to this amazing woman for inspiration. With God's help, you, too, can accomplish much. He calls you to tend your home and serve your family, and you do that in so many ways. But are you doing the best you can do? I encourage you to master new skills, express your creativity, and find new ways to help. Even if you work outside your home, you can make your home even better than "home sweet home." What an awesome privilege!

Father, thank You for blessing me with a home
and for family and friends that fill it. Help
me be industrious and cheerful as I encourage
and serve everyone who comes in. Amen.

A Faithful Steward

From basic necessities to cars, from supporting causes to vacations, the way we handle money reveals a lot. What has God entrusted to you? Do you have food in your cupboards and decent clothes for the family? Are you able to buy some luxuries, such as jewelry and going out to dinner? Financial responsibility is part of what God calls you to. The issue isn't how much or how little wealth you have, but how faithful a steward you are of what He has given you. First John 2:15 says, "Do not love the world or the things in the world."

I encourage you to do a Bible study on the numerous scriptures that give wise advice on handling money…and put into practice what you learn. As you live for the Lord's purposes and by His principles, you'll find contentment.

Father, show me how You want me to spend my money. Open my eyes to the needs of people You want me to help. I want to find the right balance between providing for my family and helping others. Amen.

A Generous Soul

Are you nurturing a giving spirit? Are you generous with all your resources? Giving God and people your time is sometimes the most expensive…and most appreciated…gift you can bestow. Generosity also includes little touches and activities you can do to brighten someone's day, such as sending a quick note, making a cheery phone call, weeding someone's flower bed, and delivering a bouquet of wildflowers.

I remember clearly the day I assessed my spiritual life and decided I needed help in this area. So I prayed…and continue to do so. Every day I ask God to open my eyes and my heart and to bring to my knowledge the needs of others. I consider it fine-tuning my heart to God's Word, God's ways, and God's grace. With His help I can meet the needs of others and reach out with His love. Why not make this one of your goals?

> *Father, show me the big and little ways I can*
> *share my resources, including my time. Help*
> *me think of others before myself when I have*
> *free time and some spending money. Amen.*

The Right Path

J ust relax. Go with the flow." We definitely live in a time that honors looseness. But that's not necessarily what being a woman after God's own heart is all about. We're to be the righteous saints of a righteous God. That doesn't mean we're perfect, mind you, but we are righteous in Christ: "By one Man's obedience many will be made righteous" (Romans 5:19). This means we're to be honorable and trustworthy and to follow God's precepts, even if that means running counter to the "easy" way, the "popular" way, or the "don't get uptight" way.

God wants us to walk His paths. And He tells us in His Word how to do so. He also clearly spells out what He considers right and wrong. How blessed we are to have a God who cares for us and guides us!

Jesus, give me the courage to stand up for You and what You say is right. Remind me that You are my Guide so I don't get caught up in something or choose to ignore a situation that doesn't honor You. Amen.

Praise God!

I'm so glad you're God's friend, that you have the promise of His blessings in your life. In Psalm 16:11, David says of God, "You will show me the path of life; in Your presence is fullness of joy; at Your right hand are pleasures forevermore." God will never fail you or change His mind about you. In His loving care you have a shelter in the storm and a haven when life bats you around. In His loving care you can have a generous heart because He provides abundantly. Use Psalm 23:6 as an affirmation of what you know to be true: "Surely goodness and mercy shall follow me all the days of my life; and I will dwell in the house of the LORD forever." Praise His holy name!

*Jesus, I praise You! You've given me many
astounding gifts and provided for and watched
over me in countless ways. You are so wonderful,
so powerful, so mighty, and so everlasting.
And You love me. Amazing. Amen.*

A Heart for Hospitality

I'm the kind of gal who has a refrigerator filled with bottled water, a few pieces of fruit, and a Diet Pepsi. Entertain? I don't think so!"

Are you like my friend? I'm hoping you'll reconsider! There are so many people around you who need love, friendship, support, and a relaxing time. Begin nurturing relationships by cultivating the art of hospitality (Romans 12:13). Then open your heart and home to others. And don't worry if your home isn't perfect. As long as it's tidy, you're good to go! Pick a time, invite guests, and plan a meal or tasty snacks. Involve your family and prepare in advance to lessen stress. Pray about your gathering and then follow through. And most of all, be flexible and have fun! Your guests will be blessed...and so will you.

Jesus, I'm excited about this idea! Guide me in the next week or two as I think about whom to invite, when to have the gathering, and what I need to do to prepare. Help me stay focused and not get overwhelmed. Amen.

Managing Money

When it comes to finances, ignorance is not bliss. If you're married, do you and your husband share financial information? Are you both aware of income and expenses, home upkeep, taxes owed, and such? If you're single, do you track what comes in and what goes out? How can you hope to manage your finances if you don't know what you've got? Managing money, like any other discipline, starts with daily knowledge of your financial condition. We can't be casual about this matter of money because it's not ours! The money is God's. And if you're going to be someone who abounds in the grace of giving (2 Corinthians 8:3-7), you need to know your resources. It's a measure of your spiritual maturity. It's a discipline that makes you the woman you want to be.

Father, thank You for blessing me with what I need. Give me wisdom to carefully manage the resources You've given me so I can use it to provide for the people I care about and the causes You put on my heart. Amen.

Trust Him Fully

How can she be so mean? What did I ever do to her?" If you're facing this situation right now, I'm so sorry. Unfortunately, we're going to have difficult relationships all our lives, especially with those who don't know Christ. That's the nature of the fallen world we live in. But our hope and strength lie in Christ!

I have a question for you: If God is on your side, does it matter who is against you? Please don't mistake this for a lack of caring or understanding. I know it's not easy to be attacked. One thing I do for encouragement is turn to great hymns. In "Like a River Glorious," by Frances R. Havergal, the words are so appropriate: "We may trust Him fully all for us to do. They who trust Him wholly find Him wholly true." Trust Him, dear friend. He will comfort and protect you.

Father, relationships can be so hard, and my feelings get easily hurt. Help me respond to negativity with Your grace and mercy. Comfort me with Your love. Amen.

Be Bold!

People should never doubt where our faith lies. We're not secret agents. No way! Along with our friendliness and genuine concern and caring actions, we're to be bold. We're to be outspoken about our faith in Jesus Christ. And we should faithfully pray for opportunities to introduce our friends to the Savior. There's no greater gift than sharing the salvation offered through Jesus. It was the apostle Paul's desire "that God would open to us a door for the word, to speak the mystery of Christ" (Colossians 4:3). Paul wanted to declare Christ openly and to as many people as possible.

I encourage you to study God's Word and meet with other Christians so you can be prepared for questions people may have regarding Jesus. You don't have to know everything, but be comfortable with a few facts about your faith in Him. Then reach out with the true gospel!

Father, I want other people to experience Your love and have Your promise of eternal life through Christ. Show me people I can minister to, help me be prepared, and give me the words to speak. Amen.

Set Life Goals

Is setting goals a challenge for you? Try it! God's servant Paul had goals. He tells us in Philippians that he was energized to "press on" to gain God's prize (3:14 NASB). Setting goals will help turn your dreams into realities.

Several years ago Jim and I wrote out lifetime goals we believed would place God and His priorities at the center of our lives. And would you believe it? We're still following those goals! Why don't you jot down some ideas and mull over your gifts, your priorities, your lifestyle? Ask God for His wisdom and direction. Seek input from mentors and those closest to you. Then formulate some goals and set out on your life journey. And remember, your goals will adjust over time. Just keep your eyes and heart on Jesus for continual guidance.

Father, setting goals is intimidating. But I know they'll help me stay focused and be more effective in serving You. Give me Your wisdom and guidance as I set my goals…and help me to carry them out. Amen.

Your Spiritual Gifts

One of the best ways to discover your gifts is to ask God about them. When you're in the Word, for example, the Holy Spirit will show you ideas for service and ministry. People will come to mind, as will ideas for how to minister to them. I know a woman who's actively building a "Barnabas ministry" based on Acts 4:36. It's a ministry designed to encourage people who are suffering and need support by linking them up with others who have walked through their trials. Another friend operates what I call "Judy's Soup Kitchen." A nurse and cancer survivor, Judy knows just what's needed when someone's ill. So off she goes with her warm ways, her warm soup, and a batch of encouraging scriptures. Faithfully read your Bible and start developing your gifts!

Heavenly Father, You've given me gifts so I can serve Your people and encourage them in Jesus. Open my eyes to what You've given me and show me how to use my gifts for Your glory. Amen.

Why Seek Peace?

Wﾠhat I need is rest. About a hundred years ought to do it!" Don't we all feel this way at times? If I asked you to fill out a survey with one of the questions being, "What causes you to seek peace?" how would you answer? I responded to this question quickly: busyness. It's number one on my list. There's always just "one more" of something to do. Responsibility is next. Tension is on the list too. Stress drains my energy. I'm sure you have your own list of feelings and activities and issues that make you crave peace. Here's the good news! Psalm 23:2 says, "[God] leads me beside the still waters." Still waters! Can't you just feel it? God knows your need for peace, and He provides it. He ensures the restoration and calm you need to continue fulfilling His will for your life.

Father, replace my stress with Your peace and
contentment. Renew in me the joy of life and
service to You and those around me. Amen.

Be Generous

I vividly recall the day I began praying to be more generous. After assessing my spiritual life, I discovered I could use improvement in this area. So every day I ask God for opportunities to give. I pray for open eyes and an open heart that will recognize the needs of others. And God began to fine-tune my senses. Jim and I have been blessed to minister to many people through teaching, speaking, and writing. We also love to privately and quietly assist when we can.

The amazing results are that people have heard the good news of Jesus Christ, people have been helped, and some people have accepted Christ as their Savior! On top of those wonderful blessings, the Lord has honored our commitment to Him in countless ways. I encourage you to be generous with your gifts, your time, and your faith. And watch what God does through you!

*Father, You've blessed me so much. As I share
with others, keep my ego in check so that You
get the recognition and thanks. Amen.*

Experience God's Peace

God provides real peace for us...and that includes you—even if you have a screaming baby, a high-stress job, or are knee-deep in troubles. You may not be feeling much like a woman after God's own heart, but John 16:33 records Jesus saying that even though in this world you will have tribulation, you also have God's perfect peace in every circumstance of your life. So even if at this moment you aren't able to fully appreciate the truth of God's peace, it's there—and it will make itself apparent. First Corinthians 15:58 says, "Be steadfast, immovable, always abounding in the work of the Lord"—and here's the part for you today—"knowing that your labor is not in vain in the Lord."

Bless you today, and hang in there!

*Father, thank You for caring so much about
me that You know I need peace and rest.
Restore my energy and my commitment to
You and Your plan for my life. Amen.*

A Positive Attitude

It may surprise you to know that a positive attitude and the giving of thanks is willful...a choice you make. Giving thanks is a conscious decision, and it's also commanded by God. His Word tells us to give thanks always and for all things, in everything and evermore. First Thessalonians 5:16-18 says, "Rejoice always, pray without ceasing, in everything give thanks; for this is the will of God in Christ Jesus for you." That's pretty clear!

And the decision to do just that—to give thanks...no matter what...in whatever situation—has a powerful effect on your attitude. Not only that, it also has a huge impact on everyone around you. Philippians 4:7 says the peace of God that surpasses all understanding is available to you and me. Now that's something to be thankful for!

Father, even though You've blessed me so
much, I still get stuck on what's not going right
and the trials I face. Gently remind me that
You're always with me. I want to maintain
a thankful heart toward You! Amen.

Share Your Love!

This is the perfect time to tell your husband, your children, your mom, dad, sisters, brothers, and your best friends how much you love them. What's so special about today? Nothing in particular…any day is a great day to let those closest to you know how much you love them! Also encourage them spiritually. Tell them you care how they feel and what they believe. And ask God to bless your loved ones and draw them closer to Him.

I have an idea! Make a list of those who matter most to you and tell each one how much you appreciate them. Write each person's name on different days on your calendar, and on that day give them a call, write a note, send an e-mail card, deliver a small gift…your options are limited only by your imagination. Have fun as you bless the special people God brings into your life!

Father, in my busy days I forget to let people know how much I love them. Thank You for bringing them into my life. Bless them and watch over them. Amen.

Start with God

Do you wonder what to pray about or how to get started? I have a few suggestions that may help you. Start with God first: "Lord, thank You for loving me. I look around in amazement at Your lovely creation. Thank You for Your sacrifice so I can know You." Consider your relationship with Him: "Lord, what can I do today to live out the fact You are my ultimate priority?" Write down God's answers and promptings. Then ask, "Lord, what can I do today to grow spiritually? How can I prepare for future ministry?" Finish with, "Lord, what else would You have me do today?"

These simple prayers put your heart and feet in line with God and His plan.

Father, I love that I can come to You in praise...and get my questions answered. It amazes me that You care about the big and little things that happen in my life. I know You love me. Help me get over any awkwardness I feel about approaching You. Amen.

Good News!

Do you know Jesus? Is He your Lord and Savior? Romans 3:23 reveals that we all have sinned. We all fall short of God's glory. And the penalty for sin is death...spiritual death. The good news is Christ died for you (and me)! Romans 10:9 says, "If you confess with your mouth the Lord Jesus and believe in your heart that God has raised Him from the dead, you will be saved." Please take this opportunity to give your life to Jesus. Open yourself to His love and truth. Ask Him to come into your heart and be with you forever. He's waiting for you!

And if you already know Jesus, praise His holy name!

Jesus, I yearn to experience Your love. In my sin-filled heart I don't even come close to being as You are. Thank You for coming to earth and paying the price for my sins so I can know You personally. I accept Your free gift of salvation. Help me grow in You every day. Amen.

Watch, Listen, Act

There's no better time than the present to notice other people's needs and do something about them. Yes, even during your busiest times. Proverbs 20:12 says, "The hearing ear and the seeing eye, the LORD has made them both." Be watching and listening to those around you. That's exactly what God does in our lives. He watches and listens and responds in loving care for our every need. Follow Dorcas' example. She was a woman "full of good works and charitable deeds which she did" (Acts 9:36). This thoughtful lady noticed the widows needed clothes, so she acted on it and made some for them. Ask God to lead you to people who need encouragement, support, and prayer. Notice those around you and keep a keen eye out for ways you can actively help.

Jesus, surely You set up divine appointments every day so I can be used by You to meet a need. Help me watch and listen for those opportunities to say a kind word or do a charitable deed. May others see Your goodness in my outstretched hands. Amen.

Prayer Will Change Your Life

D o you have trouble praying? Are you uncertain whether it accomplishes anything? Let me assure you that prayer can change your life in ways you've never imagined. Why do I encourage you to pray? For one thing, I don't want you to miss out on a ton of blessings! Prayer increases your faith in God and eases your burdens. It opens your heart to His love and peace and encouragement on those days full of panic and stress. Prayer also changes lives—yours and the people you pray for. Prayer helps you focus on others and not yourself, which usually improves relationships. Prayer brings contentment as you commune with God. It opens the path to God's wisdom so you can be confident in making decisions. And prayer is a powerful ministry. James 4:8 says, "Draw near to God and He will draw near to you."

Father, I lift my voice and praise to You. Help me know that You're listening. Give me Your strength and wisdom today. Draw close to me. Amen.

About the Author

Elizabeth George, whose books have sold more than 12 million copies, is the author of *A Woman After God's Own Heart*® (more than 1 million copies sold) and *Proverbs for a Woman's Day*. Elizabeth and her husband, Jim, are parents and grandparents, and have been active in ministry for more than 30 years.

www.elizabethgeorge.com

To learn more about Harvest House books and
to read sample chapters, visit our website:

www.harvesthousepublishers.com

HARVEST HOUSE PUBLISHERS
EUGENE, OREGON